the 3-DIMENSIONAL VOICE

Fun & Easy Method of Voice Improvement

Joni Wilson

Blue Loon Press
San Diego, California

The 3-Dimensional Voice
By Joni Wilson

Published by Blue Loon Press
P.O. Box 15660
San Diego, Ca. 92115-5660

Publisher's Cataloging-in-Publication Data
Wilson Joni
The 3-dimensional voice: a fun and easy method of voice improvement/
Joni Wilson, --San Diego, CA : Blue-Loon Press 2000
      p.cm.
Includes bibliographical reference and index.
ISBN 0-9669883-0-2
      1. Voice culture -- Exercises. 2. Diction
      I Title. ll.. Title: Three-dimensional voice

PN4197 .W55   1999   99-60399
808.5   dc21   CIP

Project Coordination by Jenkins Group, Inc.

02 01 00 99 5 4 3 2 1

Printed in the United States of America

This book is dedicated to every student that walked through my studio door and taught me everything I needed to know about the human voice. Thank You!!

Acknowledgements

Many, many thanks to all of the people with pens and pencils in hand who help to bring this book into reality. Without their loving and patient giving of time, support and expertise the rewrite process would have been overwhelming.

A loving thanks to Bob, Sandi and David who have inspired my existence and always made me keep my feet on the ground. Thanks to Christine who brought Freeda to life, and thanks with eternal gratitude to Joseph for his constant support and encouragement. This was so much fun!

Contents

Chapter 4

Browsing Through The Voice Store:
Lets Go Shopping!!...95

Chapter 5

The Mars, Venus Voice Thing 103

Chapter 6

Emotions And Other Fearful Things

Chapter 7

Voice And The Telephone: "Hello!"

Chapter 8

Age And The Voice

Chapter 9

When To Take Your Voice To The Doctor

Chapter 10

Tuning Up The Mind, Body And Soul 193

Chapter 11

Conclusion 211

Appendix

Author Thoughts

Over the years my students have urged me to write a book and share my lifetime of studying and researching the human voice. Like those who intensely search for the meaning of life, I have been searching for the perfect voice method.

Until now, I have negated their request with a wave of my hand and a slightly sarcastic *"Yeah, the world really needs another book on voice technique."*

But the more "voice books" I read, the more I realize the world does in fact need another book on voice technique. Not a clinical book, for there are many incredible books written by doctors on the anatomy of the voice. Not a book on singing, for there are as many good books on singing as there are good songs to sing, and not a book just about the speaking voice, for again, many helpful books are already available.

What is needed is a simple book with simple exercises you can do in your car or standing in line buying concert tickets. It should have the kind of exercises you can easily fit into your, " I just don't have time to practice" everyday life. It needs to be a book explaining in *plain language* how the voice works in the real world, and it should teach you how to get the most out of your own voice so it can last for a lifetime. Most important of all, this book should teach you how to change the sound of your voice as easily as you change the station on a radio.

It needs be a book of hope and understanding, for it will be about the greatest instrument on this God created planet...

The Human Voice!

Introduction

The 3-Dimensional Voice

"I just hate the sound of my voice!" I hear that statement over and over again from new students as we play back the audio recording of their first lesson. Speaking or singing, their reaction is the same, "Do I really sound like that?"

Every day actors, speakers, singers and voice professionals spend money on head shots, acting lessons, college degrees and even cosmetic surgery looking for the perfect image to succeed and yet, they ignore the most important asset of all to a successful career, THEIR VOICE!

> **We assume we're either born with a great voice or we're not, and that's it!**

We go through life complaining about our voice and its problems, but never take the time to find out why the problems exist.

"The Human Voice" is the most fascinating, *and* the most vulnerable part of the body, and it's the one part we know the least about. Every four years when election time is bearing down on us, we listen to our otherwise sane politicians yell and scream at each other until they become hoarse. Concerts are constantly canceled because the artist has no voice left to perform.

Everyday Voice problems

Teachers, lawyers, clergy and receptionists... I work with people from all walks of life who have absolutely no idea there are easy solutions to their voice problems.

As a singer and actress, I have struggled for years believing my voice was not strong enough to serve me when I needed it most. Singing with bands four hours a night, performing in musical theater, teaching and lecturing kept my voice in a state of dysphonia (hoarseness), leaving me with a raspy, breathy voice. By the end of each working day, I could barely talk. My voice problems went on for years.

Looking for Answers.

I read every book on voice I could get my hands on. I tried method after method. The fear of nodules (a benign corn-like growth on the vocal cords), and even throat cancer were my constant companions. A few days rest would restore my voice, but the rigors of performing would always pull me right back to vocal disaster. I was afraid to commit to anything I felt my voice could not handle. My fear was ruining my career!

I always thought my experience was unique until I began teaching and found student after student facing the same fears. These fears exist in people of all professions whose livelihoods depend on healthy voices.

On good voice days I felt great. On bad voice days, I felt miserable and inadequate. I knew there had to be answers somewhere.

In my quest for knowledge, I went back to the source (the medical books), to study this part of my body I knew so little about and yet seemed to be ruling my very existence.

Going from book to book and teacher to teacher gathering information, I began to experience a great new respect for the vocal instrument. I soon learned the voice does not consist of just two tiny cords in the throat. The real vocal instrument is the entire body, and how it functioned depended on the depth of my understanding.

I was blessed with incredible teachers and guides in my own search, and every day I experience the joy of sharing what I have learned with others.

There is a bright light at the end of this tunnel, so come with me on an incredible journey exploring the most ingenious part of our human body. The more you learn about the voice, the more awed you will become at this wondrous "God Given Gift" of communication.

♪ *Please Note:*

There are certain statements in this book that are worthy of noting! They will be marked by, what else but a note! ♪ Please reread all of the blocked "noted" areas and ...

Have fun!

♪Voice Notes♪

CHAPTER 1

What Is A 3-Dimensional Voice?

Picture this...

You are facing the board of directors at last! A perfectly prepared presentation is sitting on the conference table in front of you. You're wearing the new grey suit with a great Jerry Garcia designer tie to let them know just how "cool and trendy" you are.

This is the moment you've dreamed about for the past five years. Finally a chance to show everyone in the company that *you* are the best person for the job. You've rehearsed to perfection in front of your wife, kids, two best friends, and even your faithful dog. OK, it's time. Taking a deep breath, you open your mouth to speak and out comes... *NOTHING!* Swallowing nervously, you try again... *NOTHING!* As you watch your career sinking like the Titanic, you *PANIC.*

Where is the voice that spoke so eloquently two minutes ago? How could something work so well and in a heart beat become completely useless...

Welcome to the World of the Human Voice!

Anyone who has nervously stood in front of a group to, "Say a few words," has felt the dreadful fear of "voice failure". From a mild, nervous shaking, to a total "vocal 'blowout", the experience is always uncomfortable and digs a big hole in your vocal self confidence.

You can know your facts backwards, forwards and inside out. You can rehearse your presentation until you can recite it in your sleep. You can dress to impress with the best of them. But without some knowledge of vocal technique and an understanding of how the human voice works, at any given moment, whether it be physical or physiological, the "voice grippers" can get you and ruin your greatest moment.

Before we journey into the 3-Dimensional realm of voice, let's take a look at what a "voice" is all about.

Webster's dictionary simply defines voice as:
"The ability to make sounds through the mouth."

That may not be profound, but it goes right along with all the early voice research theories. Researchers believed that in man's very beginning, the human voice was only used for grunting while eating to aid digestion. (Some people I know *still* do that!)

A definition with a little more substance would be:

"Expressed choice or opinion as in:
To voice one's opinion."

The best voice definition I have found comes from a book by Dr. Robert T. Stataloff entitled *The Professional Voice*. Doctor Stataloff states that the voice is:

"The means through which we project our personalities and influence others."

How true! If we have no voice in family matters, work or government policies, our beliefs are completely ignored and as human beings we are discounted.

I always knew the human voice was an important part of life because I made my living using it. But I never realized how drastically a life would change without the use of the voice until my father developed Parkinson's disease and lost his ability to communicate and *voice* his opinion.

My Father's Voice

My father was a proud and vibrant man with a great sense of humor. Slowly, as his battle with Parkinson's disease progressed, his ability to speak began to diminish due to the weakening of the muscles connected to the tongue and his swallowing mechanisms. With the decline of his vocal power, he lost his ability to share his wonderful sense of humor. He would try to join the conversation, but after a few patient minutes of stumbled speech, people would gently pat him on his cute bald head like a child and say, *"Now, now Joe, that's OK."*

His mind was sharp and full of glorious tales to tell, but his ability to tell them was completely gone. He was depreciated as a person and treated like a stumbling child because he had no voice!

> ## What a wake-up call that was!

There is a happy ending to this story however. With a lot of loving practice using **all 3-Dimension's of his voice**, my dad was able to restore *some* of his speech and a *lot* of the twinkle in his eye. (We never were able to grow his hair back though.)

Because of this hard but enlightening experience with my father's voice, I learned through his strength and determination, no matter how bleak the prognosis may be, the human voice is much more resilient and "fixable" than the experts tend to believe.

It was because of his work and determination, The 3-Dimensional Voice Method began to take root and blossom.

Thanks Dad!

Some Early Voice Stuff

Although early writings on the human voice date back to Hypocrites and Leonardo da Vinci, serious study developed rather slowly.

It was not until the early 1980's that extensive articles on the professional voice were published, and even then, most of the writings focused on singers and actors. The good news is, since then the study of the human voice has rapidly become a science all its own, as well it should be!

Today's studies are being done on everyday voice users, not just singers and actors whose voice problems tend to be extreme. Vocal cords are no longer viewed through a dental mirror held at the back of the tongue. We can now see the intricate workings of our own vocal cords through a tiny video camera that slides painlessly down the throat and projects images of the cords at work onto a TV screen. Now that's progress!

Although most of us are aware that we have vocal cords, I am always amazed at how many people have absolutely no idea where they are located. When I ask the question;" Do you know where your vocal cords are?" The answer is generally "Oh, in the throat somewhere." The throat has become the focal point of the voice.

WRONG!

When a public speaker wants more volume in the voice, he or she goes directly to the throat and applies force to the vocal cords. The more the cords are forced, the more pressure is put upon them. When the pressure gets too extreme, the cords simply give out from exhaustion. They react like the main fuse in a stereo system. When too much pressure is put upon it, the fuse will blow out, shutting the system down. It was designed that way, so the system could not destroy itself by permanently burning out.

The vocal cord system reacts exactly the same as the stereo system. It also shuts down when too much pressure is put upon it. *When it shuts down, the voice is gone.* It is forced to take a much needed rest so the cords will not burn out and cause permanent damage. It's a *good* thing!

When the cords are rested, back comes the voice. (There is a section on vocal cords in chapter 3 explaining this process in detail for those with Enquiring minds.)

What we are constantly demanding from our voice as professional users and everyday communicators is *vocal power.* We all want that strong voice of authority. The voice that commands attention, projects our personality, and influences others. Where in the world do we find this wondrous jewel?

Enter the 3-Dimensional Voice

We've gotten used to the every day 2-Dimensional world we live in, but when we encounter anything that dips into the 3-Dimensional realm, we find it mysterious, exciting and even a bit frightening. 3-Dimensional movies, 3-Dimensional books and even 3-Dimensional television, they all leave us a little breathless as "things" come flying out at us from the pages and the screen. The hook is, in order to see that added 3rd Dimension, we have to wear those ridiculous 3-D glasses to expand our vision.

The world of sound is not the same as the world of sight. In the world of sound, we are able to hear the effects of all 3-Dimensions at once without any added perception enhancers. A voice that can move in all three directions at once is an wondrous thing to hear.

When describing voices that please and amaze us, we use words like *deep, full and loud*. We will say, "Wow, he's got a great *deep* sounding voice." Or, "Her voice is so rich and *full*." We've all said this one, "His voice was so *loud* I could hear him all the way to the back row of the theater." On that loud note, let's get right to it!

The 1st Dimension of the Voice: Depth

That deep voice we all admire in our news anchors, radio personalities, and our favorite movie and television actors and actresses, comes from the 1st Dimension of the voice *Depth*. *Depth* is defined as,

Depth: *"Measuring the distance of anything from the top to the bottom ".*

When we think of a voice we think of the mouth, throat area, so to add depth to the voice generally means lowering the tone and adding weight to the sound. This can create vocal problems because too much weight will wear the voice out.

Using the 1st Dimension of the voice, *Depth* correctly, takes the voice all the way down to the base of the torso and all the way back up to the top of the head. In other words, the full voice is the depth of the entire human body minus the legs. Think of the body as a deep well of sound. The deeper we go in the well. The greater the area we use to create sound.

Let's Take a Dip in the Well

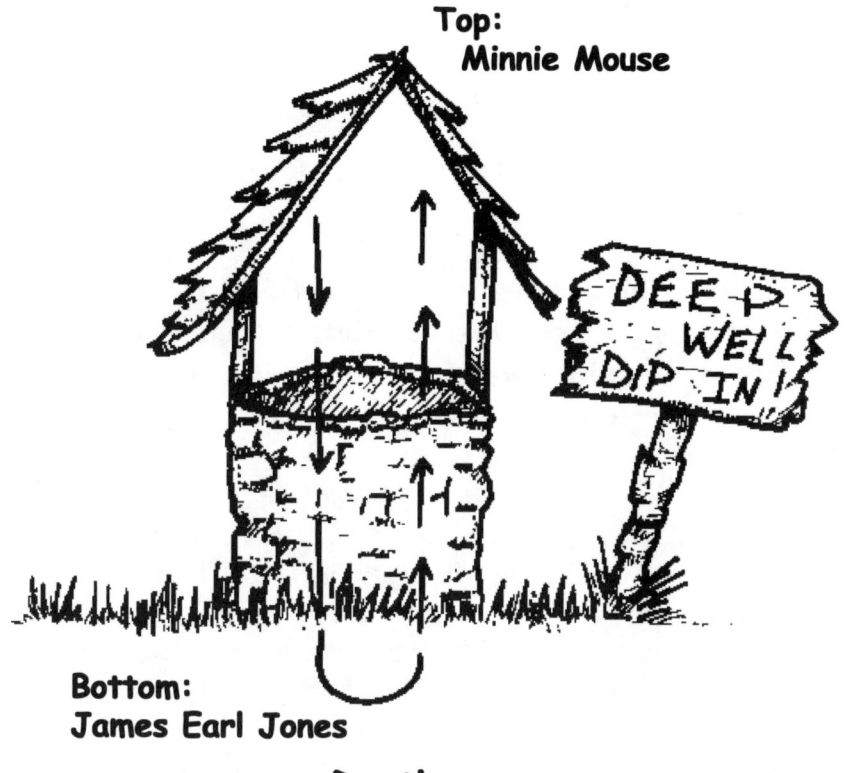

Top:
Minnie Mouse

DEEP
WELL
DIP IN!

Bottom:
James Earl Jones

Depth

This illustration shows exactly why this 1st Dimension is so important to the full voice sound. From the depth of the body comes vibration and resonance. (I have devoted a whole section in chapter three to explain exactly how to create resonance in the voice, but for now, it's only necessary to know that resonance is a series of overtones coming from vibrational sound waves pulsing through your body.)

How deep the voice resonates, depends on the depth of the 1st Dimension. In other words, a voice that resonates from the bottom of your torso, filling the lower, middle and upper body with vibrational sound waves, is a richer and fuller sounding voice than a voice that only uses the upper body.

The 2nd Dimension of the Voice: Width

A voice rich, and full of emotion, comes from the 2nd Dimension of the voice, *WIDTH*.

Width is the distance across something. It is anything that extends from side to side. Width is synonymous with the words breadth and expansion, as in: "The wing expansion of a Condor."

Width in the voice adds not only fullness (expansion) to the tone, but personality and emotion. A perfect example of vocal emotion is that bubbly, happy laugh we all love to hear in a child's voice, and haven't we all felt the voice *quiver and shake* in fear when we get up to speak? (That again.) What about the flutter of excitement in the voice when we talk to a loved one, or the emotional "cry" of a broken heart?

Just think of the 2nd Dimension as anything that creates movement from side to side. Much like a boat moving across the water. Just as the boat creates waves in the water, the emotions creates waves of sound or overtones in the voice.

Unlike the overtones in the 1st Dimension that go from top to bottom creating resonance, the overtones in the 2nd Dimension move from side to side adding "fatness and fullness" to the sound. Without the use of the 2nd Dimension the voice has a tendency to sound "flat and lifeless." Learning to access these vibrational overtones can help a dull voice "come to life."

One picture is worth a thousand words:

Now that we have the voice going up and down in the 1st Dimension, *Depth,* and side to side in the 2nd Dimension *Width,* it's time to add the final dimension to our sound.

The 3rd Dimension of the Voice: Length

The 3rd Dimension, or *LENGTH* of the voice, holds the key to that "thing" we are all seeking, power, power, and more power in the voice. Power to be heard, to command attention and respect, and most important, to have our precious words understood without constantly repeating ourselves, that's the power we are seeking.

You can think of the 3rd Dimension as projection. Anything that projects out of the mouth. How far it projects (*Length*), depends on the power and force behind it. What the sound rides out of the mouth on, is a bream of air. The stronger the air beam, the stronger the sound that rides out on it

I tell my students to project the voice out of the mouth the length of Pinoccio's nose after he has told life's biggest lie (similar to a politician at election time), or to throw the voice out of the mouth like a pitcher throwing a baseball to home plate.

How far out can your voice go?

> ♪ **NOTE:**
> *To see the 3rd Dimension, the images have to be turned to the side... To hear the 3rd Dimension, takes absolutely no adjustment at all!*

Now that you have a basic understanding of all 3 Dimensions, the time has come to put all of our "eggs" so to speak, in one basket. Or as they say in the 3-Dimensional world, it's time to put all of our Dimensions into: **One Box!**

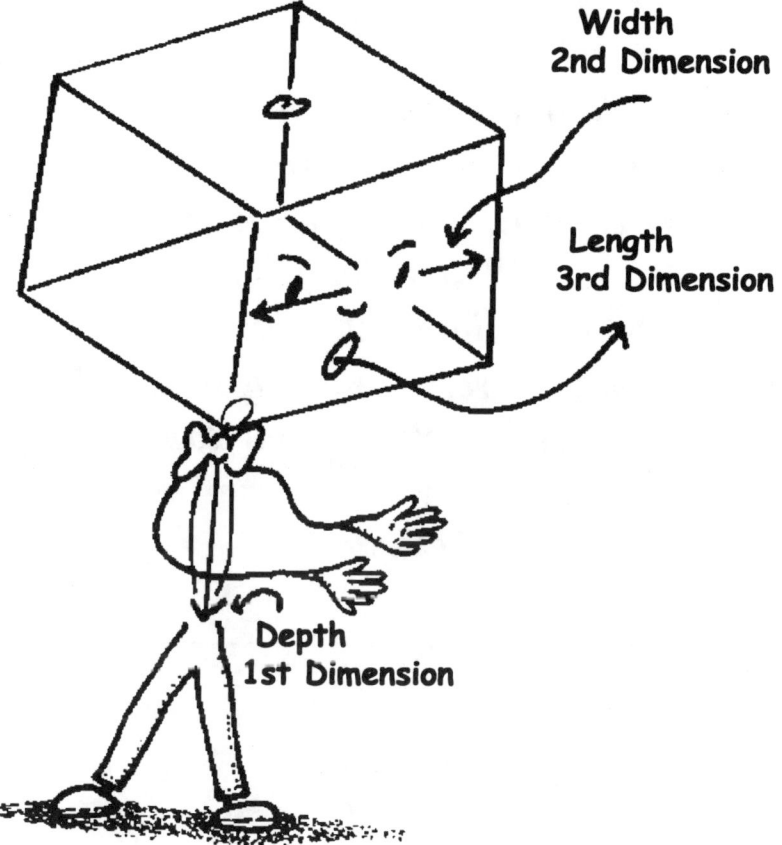

Width
2nd Dimension

Length
3rd Dimension

Depth
1st Dimension

This is the 3-Dimensional Voice at Work.

As you can see by the illustration, the voice comes up from the **1st Dimension, Depth**, expands into the **2nd Dimension , Width,** and projects out of the mouth into the **3rd Dimension, Length.** The force that moves this voice up and out is your breath (air). The strength of the breath comes up from the lower body projecting the voice out into length. (In chapter 3 *"The Big One"*, you will get a chance to do some exercises to strengthen that pillar or stream of air the voice rides out of the mouth on plus exercises using all 3 Dimensions at once.

When all 3 Dimensions are working together correctly, the result is a beautiful, power-filled voice that will last a lifetime and make you "smile" every time you hear it played back on your tape recorder or your answering machine. Let's do it!

It's time to meet Freeda ...

♪**Voice Notes**♪

CHAPTER 2

Taking The Voice Analysis Exam

If ignorance is bliss, why aren't there more happy people?

Not being happy with your voice is one thing, knowing *why* you are unhappy with it takes a bit of analysis. Most of my students are quick to complain about the sound of their voice, but when I ask what it is they don't like about it, they can't name the problem. More often than not, the part of the voice they do name, is not where the problem is. I have found the best way to pin point what needs "fixing," is to take a simple voice analysis exam.

This exam contains 20 questions. Read each question carefully to see which ones relate to your voice. A simple yes or no answer will work just fine. There are no right or wrong answers, and no grade to strive for. Your reward at the end of this test is a better understanding of how you perceive and hear your own voice. Remember, how *we* hear our voice is not always the way *others* hear it! Pencils ready? Go.

The Voice Analysis Exam

Mark YES or No to the questions that relate to your voice.

___1. Does the sound of your voice played back on your answering machine make you cringe?

___2. Do you find yourself short of breath when you talk on the telephone?

___3. Do people have difficulty hearing you and constantly ask you to repeat yourself?

___4. Does your voice tire at the end of the working day and sound raspy and weak?

___5. Do you find yourself constantly clearing your throat with a vengeance?

___6. After talking all day, does it feels as though there is a lump in your throat?

___7. Do people constantly misunderstand you?

___8. Does your voice have a nervous quiver and shake when you talk?

___9. Does your voice feel weak when you try to loudly express yourself ?

___10. Do you have frequent colds that always settle in the throat area?

___11. Do you hear your voice as high pitched and irritating?

___12. Do strangers on the telephone think you are a child? (That's a little problem.)

___13. Do strangers on the telephone think you are the opposite sex? (That's a big problem.)

___14. Does your throat feel rough and dry when you are speaking?

___15. Do you hear your voice as "lifeless" and dull?

___16. Does your voice quality sound weaker in the morning and seem to improve as the day goes on?

___17. Are you a heavy breather?

___18. When faced with a confronting situation does your voice feel tight and "squeezed" causing the pitch to go up?

___19. Does your voice sound nasal and thin?

___20. No major problems to "speak" of. You would simply like to improve the voice you have.

Now that you are done with your test, go back over your answers to see if your first response was truly the way you feel about your voice. After you have pin-pointed your problem areas, ask your closest friends what they hear in your voice and how they think it can be improved upon. Their honest observations may surprise you.

Save your answers because each one of these problems will be covered in the following chapters of this book. There are also fun exercises to do that will assist you in correcting and creating the voice you've dreamed about having.

Read On!

CHAPTER 3

The Big One
Assembling the Parts

"I don't object to people looking at their watches when I'm speaking, but I do strongly object when they begin to shake them to make sure they are still running."
Lord Birket

Like all precision instruments, the voice is composed of many parts with very specific jobs to do. Each part is an expert at its own job. When all of the parts are allowed to do their jobs without any outside interference, the result is a magnificently played vocal instrument.

Like any instrument, no matter how splendidly it is crafted, there must be a player to play it. A very skilled player who knows how to bring the most out of that particular instrument.

The human voice is a very cleverly conceived instrument. It is the only instrument you can carry with you wherever you go. It shares your life, moods and feelings. What affects you, affects your instrument. You can not pack it away in a case, or lend it to another player.

> (♪) *Let's face it, whether speaking or singing you, and you alone are the master of your own vocal instrument.*

> ♪ *To become a true Vocal Master you must know all of your voice parts on a first name basis.*

Meeting and Mastering
the Parts

THE VOCAL CORDS
(To Know Them is to ♥ Them)

Before we go any further, let's find those elusive vocal cords located *somewhere* in the throat. That *somewhere* just happens to be the *larynx.*

For those of you who just said "huh?" and haven't got the foggiest idea where or what the *larynx* is, find your Adam's apple in your neck and place two fingers on it. Got it? Good. Now swallow! The larynx is that thing that rises up every time you swallow.

It is the housing and protector of your vocal cords. Now, with two fingers still on the larynx, *yawn.* Did you feel the larynx drop down into its *yawning position?*

> (♪) *This yawn position is very important to the vocal cords. File it in your brain under "yawn position" for future reference.*

Now that you know where the vocal cords live, let's look at their position and define their job. The vocal cords or folds (as they are referred to in scientific circles), sit in the larynx directly over the windpipe. Their main purpose, over and above making sound, is to close tightly over the windpipe every time you swallow.

This closing action keeps food and liquid from getting into the windpipe. Anyone who has ever swallowed wrong (and who hasn't), knows what it feels like to have something *"down the pipe"* that doesn't belong. There is an immediate cough response which shoots air up the wind pipe with incredible strength to force the intruder out.

This is a vital life saving process!

The vocal cords sit directly over the wind pipe and they have access to all the air coming up through it. They use this air to create sound. Remember, your voice is a wind instrument just like a saxophone or a flute. If there is no air blowing through it, there is no sound coming out of it.

Here is what the cords look like so you'll recognize them when they come to visit...

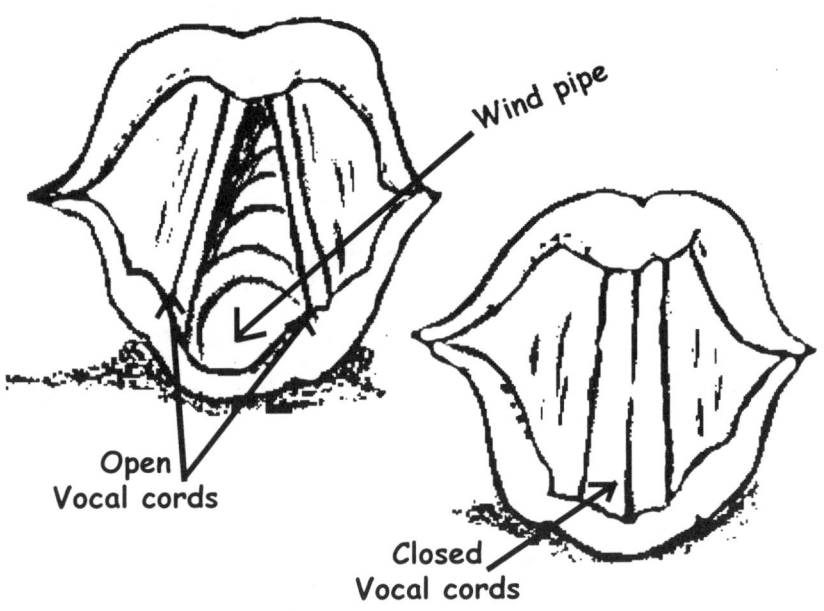

Vocal Cords (open and closed)

Now here's an exercise to do. It will help you to know your vocal cords intimately...

They are absolutely amazing !!

Your 1st Awareness Exercise:

Open your mouth in the yawn position you filed away in your brain (larynx down.) Now say ahhhhhhhhhh as you yawn. You can feel the air coming up through the cords and out of the mouth. This is affectionately called the "yawn sigh" and will be your best friend in times of vocal stress. Do it again, (larynx down) ahhhhhhhhhh. And again ahhhhhhhhh. Keep doing this during the day until you can go into your "yawn" position at will.

Because the main job of the vocal cords is to keep foreign objects out of the windpipe, *not to create sound,* no matter how hard you push to make the sound, if the larynx is in swallow position, the cords will shut tight to keep you from choking. Any sound that comes through those tightly shut vocal cords *must be forced through by you, and forcing the sound will damage your vocal cords.*

This shutting down action of the cords creates a big problem for voice users who push and force their voices. The natural tendency is to reach up for the sound by tilting the head, which in turn pulls up the chin, which in turn pulls up the larynx.

When it is in a pulled up position, the larynx thinks it is going to swallow and immediately sends a signal to the vocal cords to shut off the windpipe to avoid choking to death. While the speaker is *forcing* sound through them, the loyal cords are trying to keep the body alive by closing up tight. Guess who wins?

You can only force the cords so much before they shut down *completely.* Remember the stereo system in chapter one? It will blow a fuse before it will allow itself to burn out.

The solution to this problem is very easy when you know your vocal cords "up front and personal." *In swallow position they are closed,* in *yawn position they are open,* how simple! You cannot yawn and swallow at the same time. Just try it!!

The air *must* always flow freely through the relaxed cords, especially while you are talking. Do not allow the chin to rise up when you become excited or emotional.

The "Hhhh" Exercise:

Open your mouth in yawn position (larynx down). At the peak of the yawn, just when the air is about to come through the cords, say, "Hhhhi how are you?"... Say it on your "yawn sigh" breath. Did you feel how free the words felt as they came out of the mouth riding on the back of that "Hhhh"?

You can put an "Hhhh" in front of your vowel to gently open up the vocal cords and relax those swallowing muscles that just love to tighten the throat area. (You'll get to know them very well!) "Hhhh's" are used by singers and speakers to keep that annoying "glottal shock" sound out of the voice. Every thing from a whole "Hhhh", a half of an "Hhhh", a quarter of an "Hhhh" and even silent "Hhhh's" are all used by the skillful. Open vowels refer to vowels with no consonant in front of them like "After all". As you say those two word you will hear a slight to strong "glottal" sound. "Glottal shock is especially noticeable when the sentence begins with an open vowel.

Practice the fine art of putting your breath before your sound as it comes up and out of your mouth. Use the "Hhhh" as the bridge between breath and vowel. Open the mouth and say Hhhhh (breath) aaaaaaa (sound). Again say Hhhhhaaaaaaaaaaaaaaa. Do this during the day when ever you feel any tightness in the throat area.

Freeda will show you how to do it...

Hhhhow was your day?

Now try these "Hhhh" sentences:
- Have a ball.
- How kind of you.
- Help me do it.
- Who was that?
- Happy birthday.
- Here we go...

Make sure the "H" carries a good supply of air with it as it rides out of the mouth into the 3rd Dimension, length. The "H" is like a horse carrying the rest of the sentence out of the mouth on its back. Keep it strong and free of tension. (Remember the yawn sigh? Haaaaaaaaaaa.)

MEET MR. AND MRS. DIAPHRAGM

Last week I was delighted to see Dr. Morton Cooper, the author of *Change Your Voice, Change Your Life* on a nationally televised news program. He was demonstrating his unique voice techniques. (I have read Dr. Cooper's book several times and highly recommend it.)

This particular segment was about a man who for years could only talk in a whisper. Dr. Cooper was helping him to bring the sound back into his voice.

I watched as Dr. Cooper punched the man, and not too gently I must say, in the *abdominal diaphragm.* As Dr. Cooper punched, sound exploded out of the man's mouth and a big grin of hope lit up his face. It was wonderful to watch the human voice in action on prime time TV. I wondered at the time, how many people could actually understand the amazing process that was going on.

The voice is a wind instrument and air is the main ingredient that makes it work. Dr. Cooper's patient had an inadequate flow of air through his vocal cords. As Dr. Cooper punched the man's *abdominal diaphragm,* he manually pushed the air up from the **1st Dimension** of the voice, **Depth,** out the **3rd Dimension, Length.** (Go back and review chapter one, *What is a 3-Dimensional Voice,* if this is not clear.)

The air was pushed up the windpipe, through the vocal cords where sound is created. The sound then flew out of his mouth on a pillar of air. With each "punch" Dr. Cooper was helping the man correctly use his *abdominal diaphragm* to pump air up and through the vocal cords. Without further adieu, let me introduce you to...

The Abdominal Diaphragm
(Fondly Known as "The Pump.")

Like most parts of the vocal mechanism, the *abdominal diaphragm* has more than one job to do. This diaphragm is located underneath the lower part of the lung, and it separates the bottom half of your torso from the top half. It stretches across the entire body keeping the lower body fluids out of the lungs.

The *abdominal diaphragm's other job* is directly connected to the breath and the vocal instrument. When you breathe, this diaphragm moves up the top half of the torso pushing the air out of the bottom of the lungs, up the windpipe, through the vocal cords, and out of the mouth and nose.

The *abdominal diaphragm* works like a pump and performs just like bellows, pushing air out and sucking it back in again. Because the air pressure outside your body is different from the air pressure inside of your lungs, when the air is pushed out, it automatically is sucked back in. First a vacuum is created, then it is filled back up again.

Isn't that amazing? Take a look...

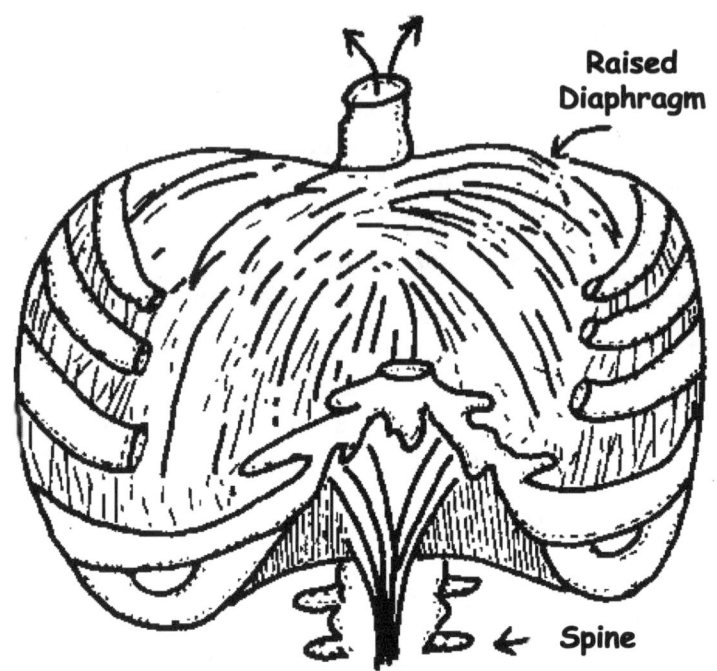

Raised Diaphragm

Spine

The Abdominal Diaphragm Front View

To actually feel the abdominal diaphragm in action, do the following exercise:

The Pant Like a Dog Exercise:

Place your finger below the sternum (breast bone), stick out your tongue, and pant like a dog on a hot day. You will feel the action of the diaphragm as it pumps air in and out of the lungs. When you first begin to do this panting exercise, you may feel a bit light headed. Stop the exercise and let it pass, then start panting again until it feels effortless and free.

In learning to use the breath correctly, I ask my students to think of the breathing mechanism as breath software we are now updating. Like any out-dated computer program, our old ways must be dumped in the trash and emptied before we can install the new breathing program. So let's trash it!

Go Freeda!

This newly programed breath data we are installing in our computer brain is actually the old original breath data we came in with. It takes us back to the first breath we took as we emerged from the womb.

To take that *first* breath, the lungs had to *first* be filled with air before any air could flow back out. Some kind of action had to occur to prime our pump before the breath could start. This action was a hard *"whomp"* on our rear. **Ouch!**

To simplify this process, think of the action of a tire pump when you pump up a tire. The pump always starts out empty. You have to put air into the pump before you can pump air back out again. *In other words, we must inhale air before we can exhale air.*

Let's take a look at the tire pump in action...

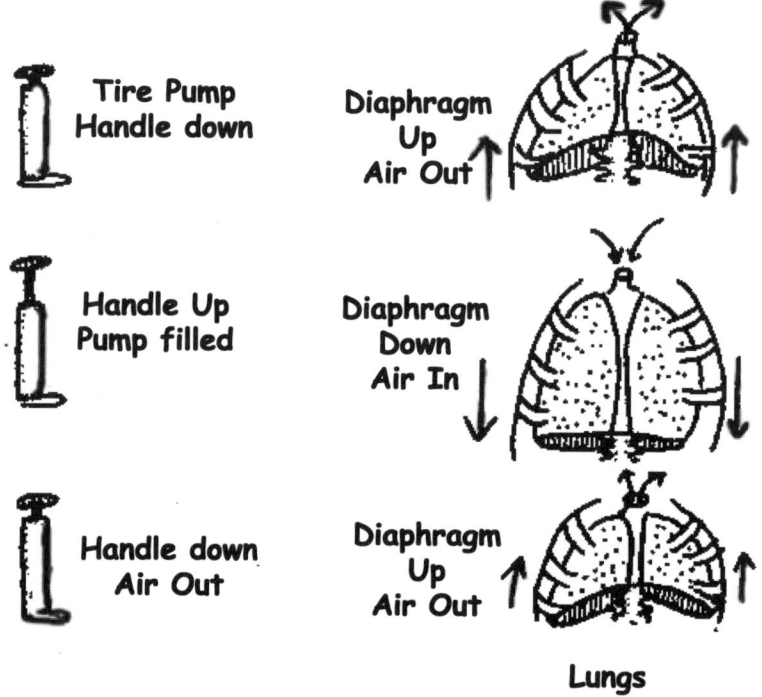

Tire Pump Handle down	**Diaphragm Up Air Out**
Handle Up Pump filled	**Diaphragm Down Air In**
Handle down Air Out	**Diaphragm Up Air Out**

Lungs

Got the picture? Good! Now start "pumping" that air!

I always find it works better to separate the air we use to breathe and stay alive, from the air we use to speak, sing, grunt, and do all of those *sound making* things. So we will now have two tanks for breath, instead of just one.

To breathe for life, we fill the large tank of air to capacity. When our brain tells us we are running out of air, we breathe again. It's one of those involuntary things we don't think about, we just do it. Our basic instincts tell us: "No breath, no life."

Our voice breath tank, on the other hand, must be *controlled* to operate efficiently. When we learn to breathe correctly for the voice, we take in the exact amount of air we need for that particular vocal task. In other words, we take in what air we need instead of filling a whole tank with air and jamming the excess up against our vocal cords.

Sometimes we only need enough air for one word. How much breath does that take? Certainly not a tankful!

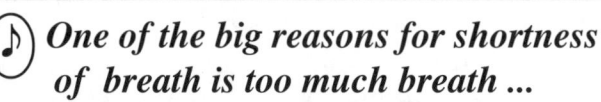

> ♪ *One of the big reasons for shortness of breath is too much breath ...*

Excess air forced up against the vocal cords restricts the easy flow of air and causes major problems in the sound of our voice. (More on that later in the chapter.)

Short relaxed breaths are always your best bet for speaking. Once again, do the panting exercise, only this time apply it to the speaking voice.

My Favorite Panting Exercise:

Place your finger on the abdominal diaphragm (You should be getting very familiar with this "spot"). Stick out your tongue and pant like a dog. Feel the pulsating action of the diaphragm under your fingers. IMPORTANT! Always start with an inhale to "prime your pump". If you have trouble doing this, get someone to "womp you on the rear." That'll get you started.

You will find it easier to exhale (send out the air), than to inhale (bring it back in). This in/out action is governed by the *strength of the diaphragm.* Since *you* have been doing the job of the abdominal diaphragm for most of its life, the muscles it (the diaphragm) uses for this job need to be strengthened. Remember, this was the original pumping action of your first breath:

> ♪ **Remember, this is the way you were BORN to breathe.**

As stated earlier, but *well worth repeating,* the body is designed so the air pressure inside your lungs is different from the air pressure outside your body. When the diaphragm pushes the air out of the lungs (exhalation) and drops back down into place (inhalation), it creates a vacuum in the lungs which is instantly filled with outside air. You don't even have to breathe. The mechanism breathes for you! Let's continue...

We have trained ourselves to breathe by lifting our upper body and filling the smaller top portion of the lungs. This action stops the natural action of the diaphragm from filling the larger lower portion of the lungs. No wonder we have trouble breathing when we speak. Using only the top of the lungs leaves us with an inadequate supply of breath in our vocal breathing tank. How did our breathing get so confused? As children we are the great imitators of life. That is how we learn. If those around us are breathing incorrectly, who is going to teach us to breath correctly? It generally begins at the age of two when some well meaning adult tells us to "stand up straight and take a deep breath." From that moment on, we think breathing is *our* job. **Wrong!!**

You now know, that the voice needs air to do its job right, and the strength of the air determines the strength of the voice. I often refer to the lottery balls that spin energetically on top of a pillar of air. If the air flow is decreased, the balls will fall accordingly. If the air flow is strong, the balls keep spinning on top of it. The same is true of the human voice. Remember, the 3rd Dimension of the voice is *Length.*

Test question:
"How do we get length in the voice tone?"
If you answered:
"By lengthening the breath."
You just got an A+.

In Review:

The abdominal diaphragm is the pump that pumps the air and projects the voice out of the mouth. On the TV show mentioned earlier, Dr. Cooper pushed on his patient's abdominal diaphragm, manually forcing the air up through the vocal cords and out the mouth. This action created vocal sound for a man who, for years, had no sound. It works!

An Exercise for You to Try:

Put the fingers of both hands on the abdominal diaphragm and open the mouth in a yawn position. Inhale the air, than say as you exhale the air, "haaaaaaaaaaa" manually pushing the diaphragm, with your fingers, in toward the spine for as long as air comes out of the mouth.

When there is no more air, and what comes out begins to resembles a "death rattle," slowly relax the pushing and allow the diaphragm to drop back down and suck the air back into the lungs. You may experience some dizziness, stop for a moment, and let it pass before you do the exercise again. You can do this throughout the day to strengthen the diaphragm.

As the diaphragm becomes stronger, the dizziness will pass. Do not let the diaphragm pop out. Allow it to slooooowly pump the air back in.

This exercise will help you to give the action of your breathing back to its rightful owner... The Abdominal Diaphragm. Now let's meet:

The Pelvic Diaphragm
Mr. Compressor to You!

Although you may not even be aware there is such a thing as a pelvic diaphragm, you are constantly using it as you go about your day.

You use the Pelvic Diaphragm to compress every time you:

- **Sneeze**
- **Cough**
- **Lose your lunch (sorry about that).**
- **Have a baby**
- **Cry and sob**
- **Feel constipated (sorry about that, too).**

The pelvic diaphragm acts as a compressor when something needs to be expelled or ejected from the body. Exactly what is a compressor you ask? Webster defines compressed as:

> **"To press together, squeeze, force, urge or drive something into a smaller compass or boundary. To condense."**

Because the main ingredient of the voice is air, what we are compressing here is air! Compressed air is:

> **"Air reduced in volume by pressure held in a container. The force with which it expands when released is used to operate various mechanisms."**

In this instance, the mechanism is the "Human Voice." We are using compressed air to power the human voice. Now that's impressive! It's time to meet your compressor:

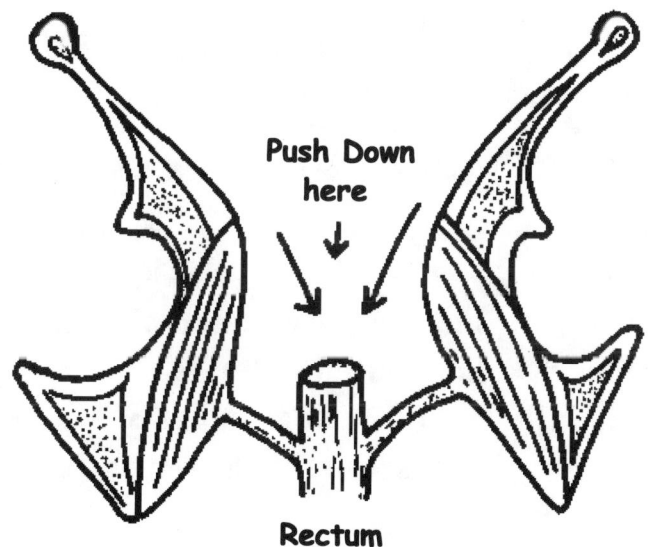

Push Down here

Rectum

The Pelvic Diaphragm

Compression Awareness Exercise:

To feel the action of the pelvic diaphragm, fake a big sneeze, Ahhhhh choooo, and feel the pressure on the rectal area. (If you can't find it, see the illustration on page 49 for location.)... Now cough... COME ON... Make it a BIG one ... Can you feel the pressure, pushing down on the rectal area yet? ... Now let's have a big sob, "Ohhh noooooooooo." You will again feel the pushing down action on the pelvic diaphragm located at the base of the rectal area... If none of this works, just push down as if you were having the world's worst case of constipation. *That will get it going!*

Like any good compressor, the *pelvic diaphragm* compresses (reduces), what is being projected out of the body. Speaking or singing, the voice is definitely a *projectile* as it travels up the pipe and out of the mouth.

This compressed air power is so strong, researchers have clocked a human sneeze at 100 miles an hour. It is powerful enough to dislodge anything caught in the throat. Why, it can even push another human being right out of the body.

♥ **GOD IN ALL OF HIS WISDOM knew we humans were a bunch of "wimpy babies," so he created a device to keep us from injuring our vocal cords when we "cry our hearts out." That wonderful device is:**
The Pelvic Diaphragm!

The Weeping Awareness Exercise:

The next time you are crying your eyes out, stop for a moment and observe the action of the pelvic diaphragm. (Oh sure.)

As hard as you sob, there is only so much sound that is allowed to come through the vocal cords. If the sound were allowed to blast through with its "full force", it would rip the cords to pieces. Compressing that force, keeps the vocal parts in line, even in an emotional frenzy.

It can be very frustrating when you want everyone in the next room to hear how miserable you are. But look at the bright side of it, compressing that sob is much healthier for the voice.

Now doesn't that make you feel a whole lot better?

Looking for Vocal Power

We are all looking for increased volume in the voice. One of the main causes of a weak voice is the constant pushing on the vocal cords to create that volume.

The actual source of this power we all seek is located a long way from the vocal cords. As a matter of fact, it is located at the opposite end of the body. The power we want is in the pelvic diaphragm. The trick is to get that power under our control and to be able to use it as we need it.

Football players in a huddle must learn to project their voices above the roaring crowd. Actors must learn to project the voice while keeping the vocal cords relaxed so the voice will not quiver and shake. Opera singers must learn to control vocal volume as must all people who depend on a strong voice to make a living.

What about the mother of three little ones all going in opposite directions? She certainly needs plenty of volume to be heard when they are in jeopardy. To be able to use this power correctly would improve all of our lives enormously. It takes two to tango so...

"I Now Pronounce You Mr. and Mrs. Diaphragm!"

Now that we have met them individually, let's put these two diaphragms together in blissful harmony, using the *pelvic diaphragm* for power and support and the *abdominal diaphragm* to pump the air, do the following exercises.

♪♪ *Double Note Alert!*
In working with the pumping action, if you should become light-headed always stop and let it pass before you pass out.
As the muscles get stronger, the light-headedness will occur less and less.

The Pelvic and Abdominal Diaphragm Exercises:

Place your finger tips on the abdominal diaphragm, (you know the spot). Now push down on the pelvic diaphragm as if you were very constipated... (sorry, I could have said like pushing out a baby but you guys would not relate)... Say "hut, hut, hut," like the football player in a huddle.

You will feel the jumping of the abdominal diaphragm under your fingertips as it pumps the air and the pushing down action of the pelvic diaphragm in the rectal area as it compresses the air. Take note, and feel this action as the sound bursts out of your mouth. The harder you push on the pelvic diaphragm, the stronger the burst. Now slow down the process... keeping the sound steady as it comes out of the mouth. Huuuuuuut... Do this exercise until the pushing action of the pelvic diaphragm is well under your control. Remember to keep doing the panting exercise everyday to strengthen the abdominal diaphragm.

Using the same action, this time change the word from "hut" to "hey" as if you were yelling at someone in the next block! Be strong! Keep the air flow steady as it comes out of the mouth. If you need more volume, push down harder on the pelvic diaphragm.

Always Remember:

1. Do not push for volume
   in the vocal cords!

2. The sound is always projected
   and comes out of the mouth
   into the 3rd Dimension, length.

3. Only by lengthening the AIR
   can you lengthen the SOUND.

Pelvic Diaphragm
Push down

Think of the action of
a tennis ball. The **harder**
you throw it down to
the ground, the **higher**
it bounces back up.

> ♪ *You can only control the tennis ball*
> *when you throw it down. The bouncing*
> *back up action is NOT in your control.*

The same principal is true of the human voice.

Just like the tennis ball, as you push down on the pelvic diaphragm the voice will bounce up. Did you ever do the "Strong
man" test at a county fair? You hit down on a designated spot
with a big hammer to ring a bell at the top and show everyone
how strong you are. The harder you hit down with the hammer,
the further up the ball goes until it rings that bell. If you are very
strong, you can hit down hard enough to ring that bell and win
the grand prize. (And a few admiring looks from those watching
you.)

The voice is the ball that travels up towards the bell, and the
bell is the beautiful ringing tones that come out of your mouth,
The pelvic diaphragm is the "X spot" that you hit and you, as
always, control the hammer. The more you push down on the
pelvic diaphragm (think "big time" constipation and puuuush),
the more compression is in the air that travels up the body, past
the breathing track, through the vocal cords and out the mouth.
In other words, the stronger the push down on the pelvic diaphragm, the stronger the air will move up the vocal track. The
stronger the air behind it, the more powerful the voice becomes.
In the singing world, it's called "support". In flying it's, "The
wind beneath your wings."

The Prize

The grand prize you will win when you "hit" the bell at the
top, is a powerful, long lasting voice. As you proudly carry that
prize throughout your lifetime, people will ask you how you
happen to have such a wonderful voice. You can look them in the
eye, smile and say, "It's a bit like playing tennis with a digestive
problem at the county fair."

Let's move on.

TAMING THE WILD JAW

"You are an acoustic instrument... *Open that mouth!***"** I repeat these words over and over to my clients every day. When someone comes in asking for more power and volume in the voice one thing that stands in the way like a sentry guarding the family fortune is the all powerful and mighty...

> # Jaw!

The jaw has a definite mind of its own. It often behaves like an out-of-control child who decides that it knows best and completely ignores any given instructions. No matter how much I coax and beg someone's jaw to relax its grip, it stubbornly refuses to open wide enough to create the amount of space needed for a good, full vocal sound. There are two elements needed to make this vocal instrument work. One is air, because voice is a wind instrument, and the other is space, because it is also acoustic. It is the jaw that controls our "space station", which happens to be the mouth.

> (♪) *A big chunk of our emotional stress accumulates in the jaw area.*

The words "tight jawed" are often used to describe an apprehensive, no-nonsense kind of person. This tight jaw tension can cause **TMJ** (*Temporal Mandible Joint Disorder*), leaving many people afraid to open their mouths for fear the jaw will click out of its socket and stay there forever.

Most people I have worked with, myself included, at some time in their lives have experienced mild to severe jaw problems. Even a simple yawn gets stifled for fear of *"jaw lock"*.

In my years of working with voices, I have found that having an understanding of how the jaw works and then applying very specific exercises will help to release the stress and teach a tight jaw how to relax.

Let's take a look at the working parts of the jaw area. This includes the chin, the neck muscles under the chin, the back of the tongue, and the socket in front of the ear lobe The following illustration will help you to visualize relaxed jaw. You will notice how the jaw drops down from the area in front of the ear lobe.

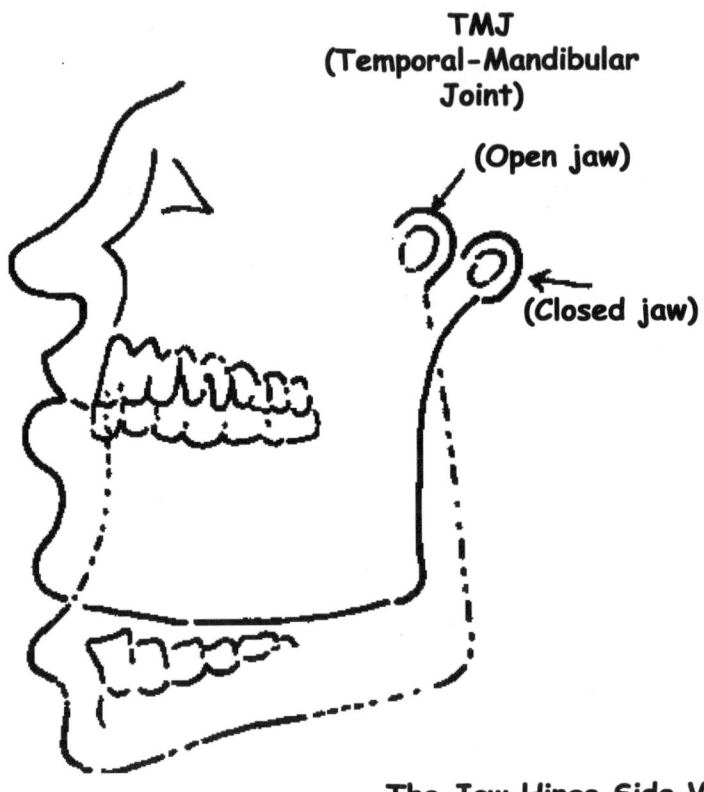

**TMJ
(Temporal-Mandibular
Joint)**

(Open jaw)

(Closed jaw)

The Jaw Hinge Side View

We have all had conversations with older folks whose strained voices are barely audible. This is the final effect of the jaw area under the chin tightening its grip, and causing the larynx to rise up. (Remember, the action of the vocal cords is to shut down when they think you are going to swallow.)

There are a group of muscles under the chin area called *strap muscles* (mylohyoid muscles for all you left-brainers). To keep from getting too clinical here, just think of the muscles under the chin as the *swallow guys*. (If you want a more detailed evaluation of this area, I suggest you visit the human anatomy section of your public library or read Robert T. Satloff's book *Professional Voice*.) Along with connecting to the larynx, these muscles are also connected to the swallowing action of the tongue.

When an older person speaks in that strained voice, you can actually see the strap muscles at work in the neck pulling the larynx up and out of its relaxed position. This action results in a pulled, strained-sounding voice. Take a look at the following illustration:

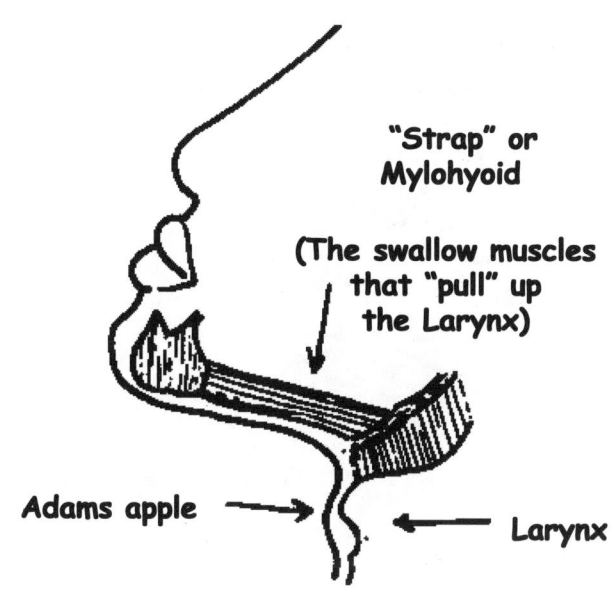

"Strap" or Mylohyoid

(The swallow muscles that "pull" up the Larynx)

Adams apple ⟶   ⟵ **Larynx**

Mylohyoid Muscles Side View

In the chin/neck area there are actually two sets of muscles at work doing two specific jobs that counterbalance each other. One group of muscles swallow (larynx up), while the other group of muscles yawn (larynx down). Remember, it is impossible to yawn and swallow at the same time. Just try it!

Using the knowledge you have now processed through your new *vocal software,* you will immediately deduce, vocally speaking of course, that those swallow guys are the *bad guys* and the yawn guys are the *good guys.* To recognize them (they don't wear good guy, bad guy hats), here is an illustration:

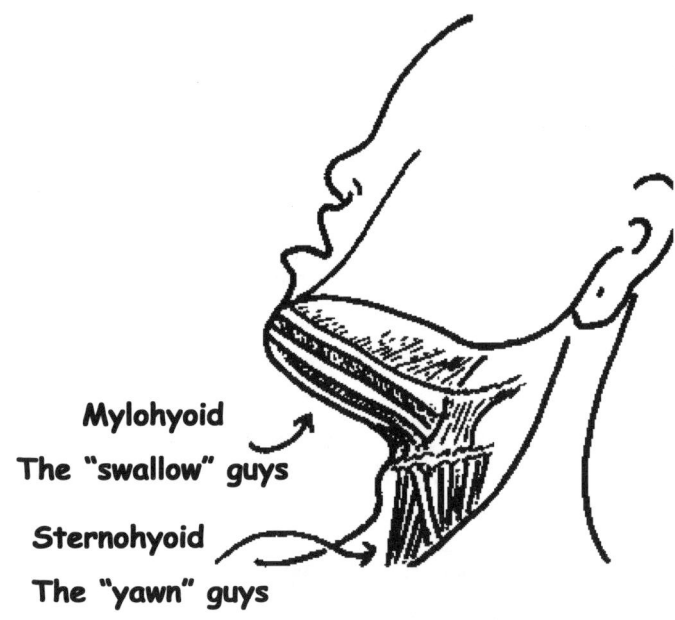

Mylohyoid
The "swallow" guys

Sternohyoid
The "yawn" guys

The Swallow and Yawn Guys

All of the jaw parts interact with common goals:
- **To open the mouth for food to enter.**
- **To yawn for air to exit.**
- **To chew (both words and food).**

When any one of these parts stubbornly refuses to cooperate, the whole system must compensate for the culprit. This throws the entire process off balance. In other words, when that "wild jaw" refuses to open, for whatever reason (physical or psychologically), *it must be trained to open up* for the good of the vocal instrument.

Retraining the Jaw Exercise:

Place your fingertips on both sides of the jaw at the ear lobe level. Find the indented place that houses the mandible joint. Now, drop the jaw in a yawning position. You will feel the jaw slide or "pop" out of the ball joint socket as the jaw drops down. The ideal jaw drops straight down as in the following example.

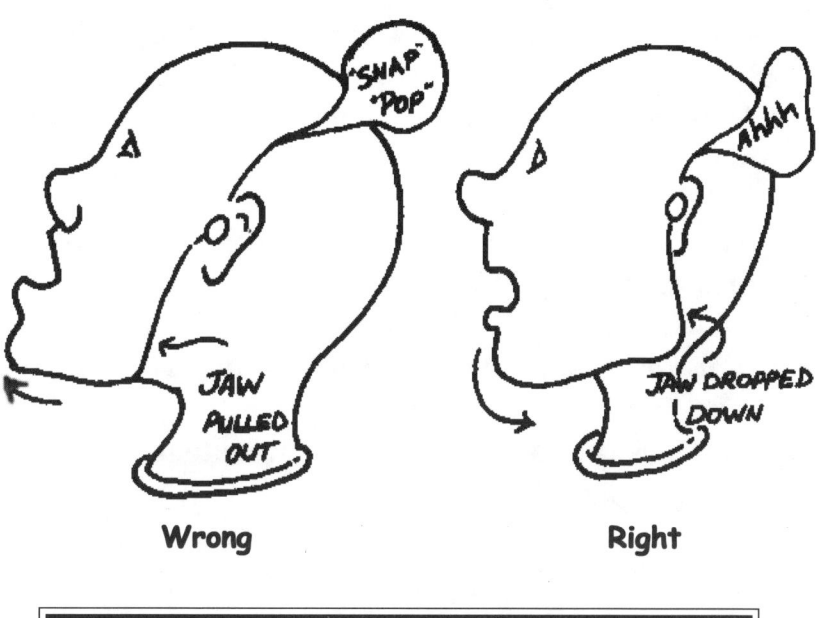

Wrong   **Right**

♪ *Do not allow the chin to "jut" out.*

The jaw muscles are all connected to each other. When the chin "juts" out, the ball joint (mandible) by the ear lobe, pulls out of its socket, the larynx goes up to swallow and the vocal cords close. No wonder we have voice problems!

When you understand how important to your vocal health a little thing like *how to drop the jaw* is, and what complex problems will be created by simply letting that jaw push forward, you will begin to appreciate a good healthy voice. You will then take the time to correct the small problems before they become big nightmares.

Helpful Exercise to Correctly Drop the Jaw:

Watch how people around you open and shut their jaw when they speak. Notice those with robust voices and a hearty laugh, just open the mouth and "let 'er rip"... While those who keep the jaw tense and tight appear to be tense and tight themselves.

Buy yourself a small round hand mirror. While looking at the mouth area only, drop the jaw down into a full yawn... now slowly close the jaw. Do this several times closely watching the up and down action of your jaw. Ask yourself:

- **Does the jaw move forward instead of dropping down?**

- **Does the jaw move from side to side as it shuts?**

- **Do you stop before a full yawn for fear of "jaw lock?"**

- **Does your jaw do the "jaw dance" to the music of popping and snapping?**

- **While watching the jaw action in the mirror, slowly speak the phrase 'Drop the Jaw.'' As the jaw is gently dropped down, be sure and stay in the "yawn position." Also, be very aware of how you close your jaw. Do not let it pull to the right or the left.**

The object of this exercise is to become aware of how you drop your own jaw, then to correct the alignment of the jaw by slowly and gently training it to move *up and down,* not side to side.

My own jaw had a tendency to pull to the right side when I closed my mouth because my mouth is crooked. (As I have found most mouths to be.)

This constant pulling to the side interfered with my singing *and* my speaking voice. It also made my jaw *very tired* at the end of a long day. I practiced the mirror exercise faithfully 10 minutes a day for one month and corrected that right side pull.

Having a crooked, tight jaw also caused me to grind my teeth at night, often waking up the next morning with a very sore jaw. I solved this problem by being fitted with a *night guard* by my favorite dentist. It was one of the kindest things I ever did for my jaw. As the jaw tension became less, my voice increased its strength and endurance.

Correcting the jaw early in life wards off a lot of voice tension problems that show up later. What you do now will last a lifetime if you do it right **and** keep it up.

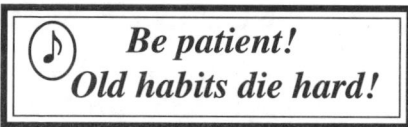
Be patient! Old habits die hard!

THE RESONATORS
Your Body's Natural Speaker System

"It Ain't Over Till the Fat Lady Sings!"

Have you ever walked into a concert hall where those large ominous speakers are sitting like sentinels on each side of the stage? Isn't the first thought that goes through your head (if you're over thirty), "I sure don't want to sit in front of those big, loud speakers!" It is our automatic response to equate *big* with *loud.*

> ♪ *The bigger the speaker,*
> *the bigger the sound.!*

Big voices bring to mind the opera Diva with a large body to hold that large singing voice. There is a great deal of truth to that observation.

> (♪) **When it comes to big voices, girth is definitely a plus factor.**

It's fun to watch the *Three Tenors* in concert. Pavarotti is a large-bodied man. Placido Domingo is also a large man. But the third tenor, Jose Carreras, is a smaller man. He works very hard to achieve the same volume and resonance as the other two who come by it quite naturally due to their body size. This is not to say you should eat that extra plate of pasta, it's just to say, *yes, size does make a difference when you are speaking of voice resonance*. The bigger the speaker, the bigger the natural sound.

The voice, riding on that pillar of air, originates in the vocal cords. It begins life as a squeak and amplifies itself as it moves up the vocal tract.

If the vocal tract were magnified many times over, it would resemble a coral reef at the bottom of the ocean floor with thousands of little sound pockets. Each one of these tiny pockets acts as an amplifier enlarging the voice as it moves up the vocal tract. When the voice reaches one of those pockets, it spins around much like sound in a speaker is *pulsed* by the speakers cone. As the sound spins, it picks up volume. With each pocket it enters, the volume increases. By the time it comes out the mouth it is full of beautiful resonance.

**To make this very important process
perfectly clear, let's follow the voice
as it travels up the vocal tract...**

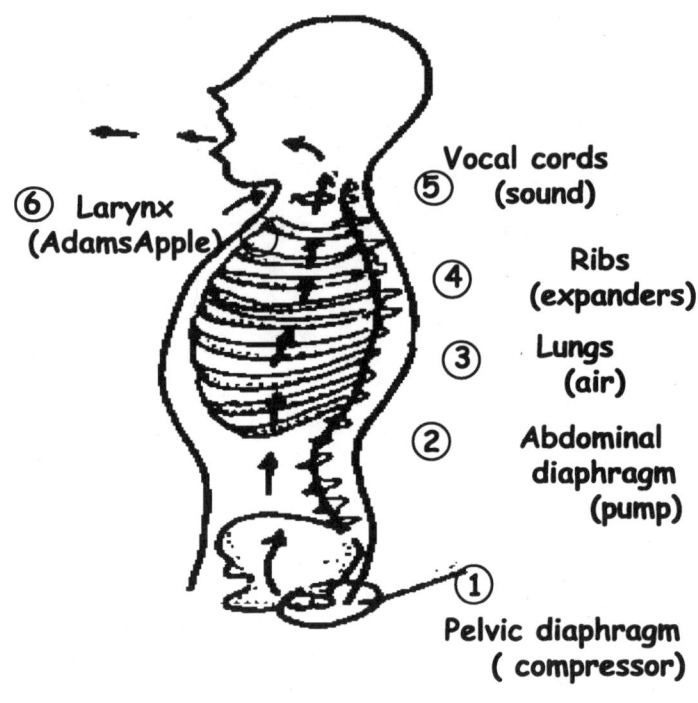

⑥ Larynx
(AdamsApple)

⑤ Vocal cords
(sound)

④ Ribs
(expanders)

③ Lungs
(air)

② Abdominal
diaphragm
(pump)

① Pelvic diaphragm
(compressor)

The Vocal Tract

The voice that starts off as a squeak, becomes warm and powerful as it fills each tiny pocket with sound on its upward journey. The biggest enemy of a beautiful, resonant voice, is tension. If the vocal track is tense, the tiny pockets will stiffen. The sound will then pass right by, bouncing *out* of the stiff pockets instead of spinning freely in the relaxed pockets.

Anyone familiar with how sound is created can appreciate the intricate workings of this human speaker system. It is important to know when panic and fear grip the throat area (the old, "I've got a lump in my throat panic-attack"), the voice bounces from side to side through the vocal tract like a ball gone wild in a pinball machine.

Without the loving benefit of the resonators, the voice comes out of the mouth tight and shrill instead of warm and full. These resonators in the vocal tract area are only a portion of the areas of the body capable of amplifying the voice in this human resonating system.

There are four other areas in the body that can vibrate and expand the sound. Take time to look them over. Each has a role in creating a specific sound in the voice. To change the tone and texture of your voice at will, you *must* know all five areas and be able to access them at will.

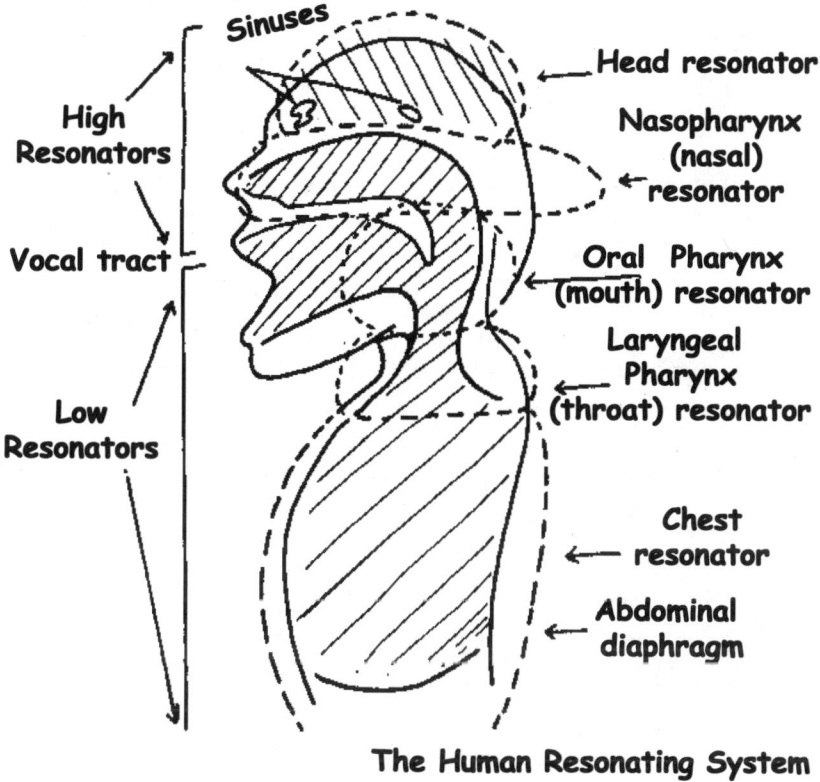

Sinuses

High Resonators

Vocal tract

Low Resonators

Head resonator

Nasopharynx (nasal) resonator

Oral Pharynx (mouth) resonator

Laryngeal Pharynx (throat) resonator

Chest resonator

Abdominal diaphragm

The Human Resonating System

Moving the voice up and down the resonators increases the volume by using the sound pockets and *not* pushing for volume in the vocal cords.

Put this sentence on your voice computer screen and keep it in front of you every time you use your voice...

> ♪ *"In creating volume in the voice, the vocal cords are definitely off limits!"*

It's obvious you cannot travel through life with a lavaliere microphone in your back pocket every time you speak, therefore to tap into your own built in sound system is vital. (This section will help those of you that checked number 3 in the Voice Analysis Exam.)

Let's travel up the resonators with the voice and get a first hand look at the road it travels. Because the voice is a *projectile,* we will start from the 1st dimension, *Depth,* and move up.

The Chest Resonator

Here is where *girth* can be a large (no pun intended) factor. Calling someone "barrel chested" refers to the roundness of the rib cage/lung area. Again, this brings to mind the large opera singer with the big voice. They (opera singers that is) are certainly the greatest example of power and strength in the human voice. There is **no** other use of the voice that takes as much skill and discipline. Tapping into the chest resonator is a vital tool for gaining big voice power.

The *chest resonator* is known for creating the lower tones. It is also used to round off and warm up the higher voice tones. To increase the lower resonance and embellish the voice, the singer or speaker expands the chest from the backbone out. This can easily be done because located between each rib is expandable material. This material is important, for as we grow in years or weight, the chest area needs to expand and accommodate our added size.

As the chest expands, a bigger housing for the lower voice resonance is automatically created. Remember, the *bigger the speaker, the bigger the sound,* and bigger is better when it comes to voice.

Rib Cage Expanders

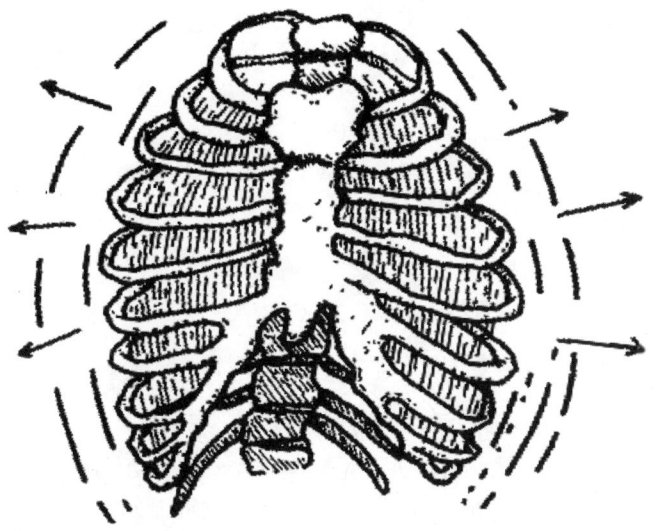

The Rib Cage

Keep in mind it is not a loud voice you are after. What you want is expansion and fullness in the voice (resonance and over-tones), which will result in a bigger, fuller sound. When volume is the object, the tendency is to push and stiffen the cords. The resulting sound is not pleasant!

Another misguided tendency is to add *weight* to the voice by speaking *heavy.* When someone says, "lower the tone of your voice," if we do not have a good understanding of exactly what that means, we automatically push the voice down on the vocal cords. Do that for a few days and you'll soon see how adding weight to the cords is too heavy a burden for them to handle, so they just "shut down." (There's that stereo system at work again.) One of the most common results of too much weight on the cords is *chronic hoarseness*. Men who try to lower their voices by putting weight on the vocal cords will find their voices growing weak and hoarse at the end of the working day.

Correctly using the resonating space in the chest area is necessary for anyone who is seeking a deeper tone in their voice. The more vibration you feel in the chest, the more resonance or bottom you have in your voice.

The voice is an instrument that needs *air* to move it and *acoustic space* to embellish it. Any increase in that space will increase the size and sound of the voice.

A Chest Resonator Exercise
to Do in Your Car:

With both hands on the steering wheel... push down on the wheel while pushing down on the pelvic diaphragm, (rectal area). From the backbone at the bottom of your rib cage, feel the material between each rib expand outward... hold it out for a count of 20... now relax. Repeat the process. Expand... hold it out... relax. Expand ... hold.. relax. Do this exercise until you can control, at will, the expansion of the rib cage.

While expanding the ribs, open your mouth into a yawn position. Say "haaaaaa... feel the rib cage expand, hold it out for as long as possible, then relax... hold it for 20 seconds to begin with and slowly increase your time.

As you hold out your "haaaa"... think of the 3rd dimension of the voice, Length. (Pinoccio's nose). Now lengthen the tone as you hold it out...

Keep doing this exercise until you feel the sound moving freely out of the mouth riding on the air. Try it soft, and try it loud. When the "ha" is free, try "ho" and "he".

The Laryngeal Pharynx
(Throat Resonator)

This area houses those precious little guys that make this whole voice thing happen, *the vocal cords.* Again, watch your big-voice-people drop their jaws to expand the area through the neck. Size is also a factor in this area, so wide necks are good mid-range voice amplifiers.

The *laryngeal pharynx* is the passageway to the lower voice resonators in the chest. If the voice resonance stops in the throat and does not dip down into the 1st Dimension, *Depth*, we will have a shallow sounding lower voice with *no* deep over tones. This can be disastrous for a man of authority.

I often think of Michael Jackson and how hard it is for me to take his acting seriously because his voice sits so high in the resonator. He does however have lower overtones in his singing voice, isn't that interesting?

♪ *To resonate properly and create warm lower overtones in the voice, the throat area must be completely relaxed!*

Just like the jaw area, this resonator holds a lot of tension, especially emotional tension like anger, sadness, fear and frustration. This is also the area that *"quivers"* when we get nervous, and it's where that *lump in the throat* is so annoying when the larynx rises up. (We *all* know that one.) *This is also where we just plain choke up.*

Knowing now that a raised larynx is the cause of most of the tension in this resonator, the task is to keep the area open and the larynx down in a relaxed yawn position. Keeping the area free of tension is often a full time job during stressful times.

Here are some simple tension relieving exercises you can do in the hotel bathroom before you give the big presentation. Do them religiously if you have a tendency to get *very* nervous.

Relaxing Exercises for the Laryngeal Pharynx Resonator:

One:
A simple neck roll is always a good starter. Drop the head gently forward and roll it first to the right all the way around, then to the left, all the way around in a circling movement. Repeat the process at least two times with the eyes closed and relaxed. Then turn the head to the right side as far as it can go, then to the left as far as it can go.

Two:
To relieve tension in the shoulder area, do shoulder shrugs. Lift the shoulders up as far as they can go, then drop them back down. Do this ten times. Be sure and drop them gently. We want to relax the neck, not build muscle.

Three:
To clear the passageway and get the larynx relaxed and down, do the "panting like a dog" exercise. Do not pass out or you'll miss your presentation. Now add a ha ha ha to your panting ... Now a he he he... Now a ho ho ho. You can feel this sound pulsating in the abdominal diaphragm area. (Use a low ho, ho, ho voice like Santa

Claus) This action will help to lower the larynx into a relaxed yawn position and warm up your pump (the abdominal diaphragm).

Four:
Remember, the raised larynx is connected to your swallow mechanism and the swallowing action is... larynx up... swallow... larynx down. The simple act of sipping water during your presentation will help to bring the larynx down at the end of each swallow. It will stay down until you hike it back up again. When you feel the lump coming up, take another sip of water to swallow it back down. Do not gulp the water. That could result in water down the wind pipe and choking. Little sips will do the trick just fine.

The Oral Pharynx
(Mouth Resonator)

The oral pharynx is the orifice through which the voice is projected into the 3rd Dimension, *Length.*

I can give you a clear picture of exactly what the *oral pharynx* looks like in two words: *Mick Jagger.* (He's the lead singer of the Rolling Stones for all of you who have been off the planet for the last 20 years.) Now that is what I call a great mouth resonator!

The mouth is the area where the bottom resonators (chest and throat) and the top resonators (nasal and head) meet. Think of it as a *sound system mixing-board,* where everything comes together and is projected out. For all of you who say, *"My voice is sooo boring,"* this one's for you!

This is a time when the word *"unplugged"* is used a lot in popular music. Unplugged means no amplifiers, just the natural acoustics of a beautiful instrument. It is very important this unplugged instrument has strong natural acoustics that can project a sound easily heard all the way to the back row of a concert hall. Good acoustics come from *space resonating sound.* You can find good acoustics in your shower when you sing in the morning. (Try this one if you haven't already. Shower singing is a great stress reliever and a perfect way to start your day.) Some spaces have natural acoustics and resonate a better sound, while other spaces resonate a flat, dull sound. The shower stall is known for good acoustics. The problem with the shower is not too many people can fit in there with you to appreciate your singing. Back to *Mick Jagger...*

Again, the acoustics of a vocal instrument have a lot to do with size and shape of the instrument. This is not to say you need a mouth the size of Mick's to project the voice, only to stress this point:

> ♪ *No matter what size the mouth is, to be heard in the back row, it must be OPEN.*

Like the acoustic guitar, the acoustic voice needs a hole. Plug up the hole in your acoustic guitar, and you'll have no sound. Close the mouth, and ditto.

For a voice to be heard, it must be projected. Most of us don't trust the sounds that come out of our mouths, therefore we keep those sounds safely tucked back inside of the mouth. This causes a dark, muffled sound in the voice. A dark, heavy sounding voice is harder to hear than a light, brighter sounding voice.

Foreign and regional accents also play a role in our voice patterns. Where we live often determines where our voice sits in the mouth. For example, a southern accent has a tendency to be a forward, nasal sound, while we who come from California have a tendency to swallow our words creating a darker sound that sometimes resembles a mumble.

Children will imitate their parent's vocal characteristics. For example, if the parents accent is stronger than the regional speech pattern where they live, the children will imitate what is predominant to their ears. It is important to gain a measure of control over where the voice sits in the mouth. For us to trust the sound that comes out of the mouth, we need to fully understand and control our own *mouth acoustics.*

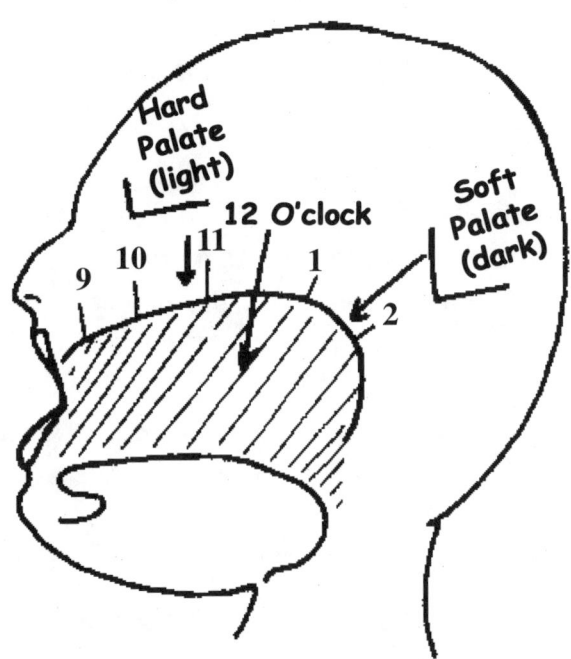

The Oral Pharynx

Take a good look at the *oral pharynx* on this page, you will notice a dial has been placed on the roof of the mouth that goes clockwise and back towards the soft palette and counter clockwise and forward towards your upper teeth.

A voice that sits in the back of the throat (soft palate area) past 12 o'clock (going clockwise) has a tendency to sound *dark,* while a voice that sits forward (in the hard palate area) toward the upper teeth at 9 o'clock sounds much *brighter.*

> (♪) *Practice the fine art of dialing your voice dark to light and light to dark with the following exercise.*

Vocal Placement Awareness Exercise:

To do this, open your mouth in a yawn position and say haaaaaaaaa... Using your finger for a dial, go counter clockwise from back to front and clockwise from front to back. Follow your finger with the voice. As it goes back, notice the darker sound, and as it moves forward, you will hear a lighter sound. Do this until your brain says; "I'll be darned, this actually works!

Freeda will now show you how to correctly dial your voice to find the right amount of brightness for your particular vocal tone.

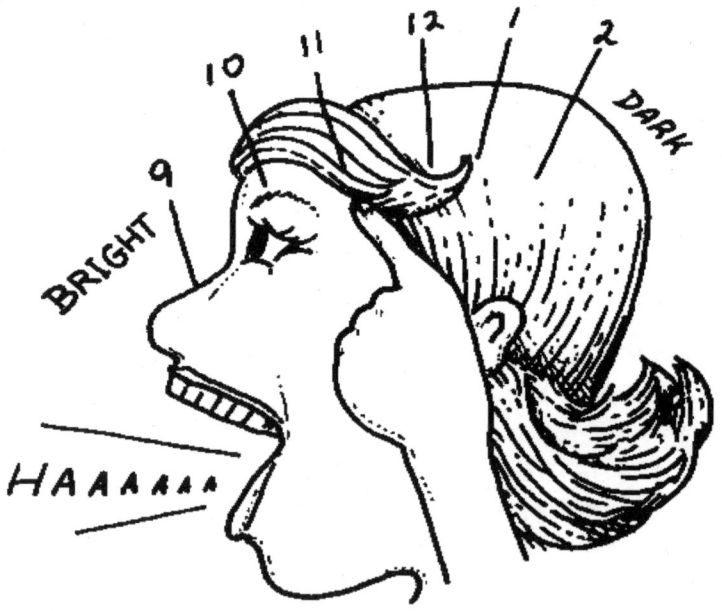

> ♪ *The oral pharynx is the place where the voice actually breaks free for all the world to hear it!*

The Nasopharynx Resonator

We laugh at the characters on TV with *whiney nasal voices* and congratulate ourselves on how lucky we are that we *don't* sound like that. We are amazed at a pop singer's high notes and secretly wish that we *did* sound like that.

> ♪ *Both of these voices come from the same place, the nasal cavity or nasal resonator located in the space between the roof of the mouth and the sinuses.*

It is the area that houses the nose. It's where the voice "buzzes" with resonance when *Frank Sinatra* or *Michael Bolton* sing. It is where *Barbra Streisand* and *Celine Dion* find all of their incredible high notes. It is also where a lot of country music lives. Most pop singers known for high, powerful notes are masters of this resonator. You will notice many of them are well endowed with *"nose girth"*. I will not say *size does matter* again I promise, but ever wonder why the pop singer, who can well afford it, does not get a nose job? The *proboscis* (nose) is a magnificent place for the voice to be and carries in it the resonance of all the higher tones. It is not just the length of the nose that fills with high resonant tone, it is also the bridge of the nose right underneath the inner corners of the eye. When someone has length and width in the nose the sound they can produce is amazing. (I have often thought of getting a reverse "nose job" just to feel the glory of the nasopharynx resonator.)

Higher resonate tones will project more than the lower resonate tones. Study the following illustration and notice how close
to the nasopharynx resonator the sinuses live. That is why we
have such a wonderful resonating voice when we have a cold.

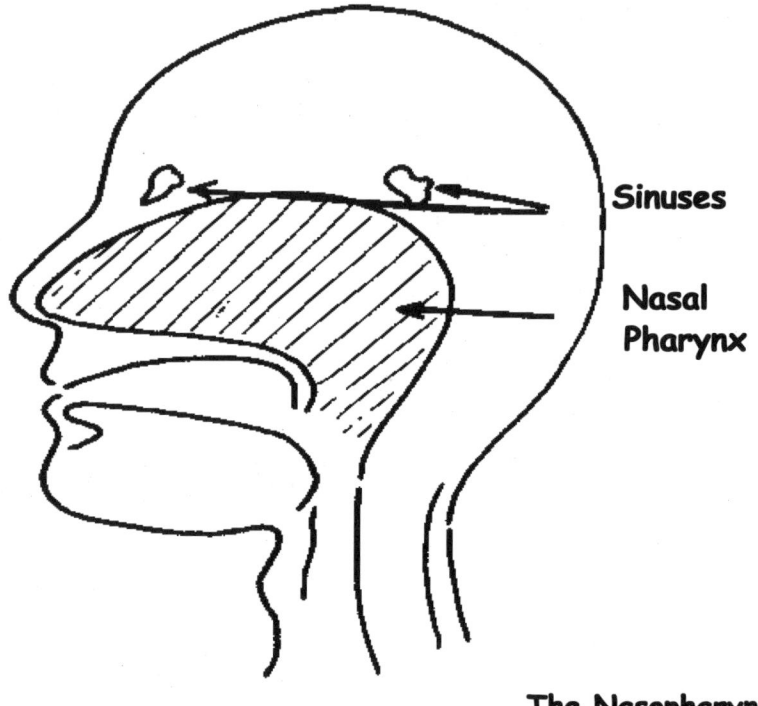

Sinuses

Nasal Pharynx

The Nasopharynx

In the speaking voice the nasal resonator is a very important
part of the full voice sound. It is the area where the *m's* and *n's*
"buzz." If we do not have resonance in this area the voice lacks
good high tone resonance. A voice without high resonance is a
dull sounding voice.

The *m's* and the *n's* are the only sounds that *can* "buzz" the
nasal cavity. Both the tongue and the lips play a very active part
in creating this particular resonance sound. The *n* uses the tongue
and the *m* uses the lips. This is one resonating sound you can
definitely feel when it's done right. Here is an exercise to help
you feel "buzzed" that's non-alcoholic.

The M and N Exercise:

Buzzing the "N"

The tongue sits in two different positions to create the "N" sound because it is actually two sounds... Eh (and) Nnnnn. On the Eh, the tip of the tongue rests on the bottom lip. On the Nnnn, it sits on the gum line of the top teeth pushing that Nnnn sound into the nose or nasal pharynx.

Ready? Let's give it a try. Eh... (tongue down) Nnnn (tongue up) again, Eh (down)... Nnnn(up). Do this until you can FEEL a resonant BUZZ in your nose on the "N."

> ♪ *A slight "wrinkling" of the nose on the Nnnn and Mmm will help you get in the buzz easier, faster and deeper.*

Buzzing the "M"

The "M" also starts with an Eh only this time, close the lips to create the Mmmm sound. The tongue again rests on the lower lip for the Eh, and stays there as the lips close for the Mmmm. Ready? Eh... (Tip of the tongue resting on lower lip)... MMMM ... Eh... Mmmm (Don't forget to buzz the Mmmm in the nose.)

Now try them both together and feel that buzz. For some it comes easy because of natural resonance in the nose area, for the rest of us, it takes a bit of work.

Begin your "buzz the resonator" program by reading any piece of text. It can be a newspaper article or a presentation you are currently working on. As you read, use a transparent marker to mark the M's and N's. You will be amazed at how many live in a few simple sentences. (There are 33 in this paragraph. Find them.) Read the paragraph out loud and buzz those M's and N's. Listen to that full, ripe, nasal resonance "bzzzz".

I have a favorite exercise I give my clients to increase their awareness and help them enter the world of nasal "buzzzz". You can do this one in your car:

Auto Awareness Exercise:

Look for road signs, billboards and signs on buildings. When you see one with an M or N in it, buzz it through the nasal cavity at the bridge of the nose (illustration on page 78).

To get this buzzing feeling in the nose, make a humming sound like an annoying fly buzzing your room while your trying to sleep. Feel the buzz in the bridge of your nose, right between your eyes. Remember, a slight wrinkle of the nose helps to find the spot. (Elvis did this all the time.) You will hear the buzz in your head and feel it vibrate or "tickle" your nose, teeth and lips. Make sure the tongue is in its proper place. Do not, I repeat, do not place any vowel or consonant in the nasal pharynx. This will result in your whole tone sounding nasal. Only buzz the M's and N's.

Practice makes perfect! If you have little or no nasal resonance to begin with (like me, I'm a Californian), it will take time and patience to get into the resonant buzz. Believe me, the end result will be well worth the time spent. Bear in mind that any ethnic or regional accents play a great role in the amount of "natural resonance" you have to begin with. You will notice in the illustration on page 78 how close the sinuses are to the nasal resonators. Remember the buzz you felt in the nose and head when you had the worst cold of your life? Recreate that feeling by duplicating the buzzing sound it made in your head. You will be well on your way to understanding and creating a good nasal resonance sound in your voice.

Here are some "Buzz" signs to look for:

Tur**nnnnn** right
Hal's **Mmmm**arket
La **Mmmm**esa blvd.
Mmmadiso**nnnn** bridge
Mmmmira **Mmmm**esa **Mmm**all
Nnno left tur**nnnn**

Now go find some of your own!

The Head Resonator

Like the chest resonator, the **head resonator** is not about making sounds in an empty space. The head space is already occupied by your brain, just as the chest space is occupied by your lungs. It is more about vibration than open space.

The head and the chest are like sub-resonators, not pure resonators. In the world of singing, the *head voice* is considered the high voice, and the *chest voice* is considered the low voice.

This tends to be a bit confusing, for a head voice without a chest resonator is shrill. On the other hand, a chest voice with out a head resonator is heavy and dull. The voice we are seeking is a full voice, with beautiful highs and lows artfully balancing each other. To achieve this full voice, sound, it is vital we know how to place it from the bottom of the chest resonator to the top of the head resonator. This involves using the 1st Dimension of the voice, **Depth**, to its fullest extent. Go back again to the illustration on page 78. You will notice that *the sinuses are in the head resonator, not the nasal resonator.* That is why when we have a head cold and those sinuses are filled with liquid, we can hear the resonance amplified loudly in our head. Water is a great conductor of sound. The more those sinuses are filled with liquid, the more head resonance we feel.

To understand where the head voice is and how it affects the full voice, think of the head as a vibrating conductor of sound. Let's clarify that with a head resonance exercise you can do anywhere, any time!

Climbing Up the Head Resonator Exercise:

Picture yourself standing on a ladder that goes from your oral pharynx (mouth), up past the nasal pharynx (nose), to the top of your head.

You are standing on the bottom step of this ladder ready to climb up one step at a time. With each step up the ladder you are going one step higher in the resonance.

Open your mouth in a yawn position placing your finger lightly on your top lip. Close your eyes and say ha... See yourself stepping up to the next rung on the ladder. Place your fingertip on the tip of your nose and say ha... Step up, moving your finger to the bridge of your head, nose. Say ha... Step up. Put your finger between the eyes. Say, ha... Finger on the forehead. ha... Finger on the hairline, ha... Now put your finger on the top of the head (which for some is the hairline) and say ha... As you move your finger up the resonators step by step, the pitch of the voice automatically follows your finger. At this point it is very important to remember that the change in pitch is created in the vocal cord area and has nothing to do with climbing up the resonators. Your vocal cords are responding to the direction you are going in your resonance and changing pitch to go with your lifted resonance.

> ♪ *The resonators only embellish the sound, they do not make the sound. That is the job of the vocal cords!*

The Articulators
("Tip of the Tongue, Lip and the Teeth")

Speaking or singing, anyone who has had professional voice training has done the *"Tip of the Tongue, Lip and the Teeth"* exercise to improve articulation.

Just exactly what is articulation, and what is the difference between articulation and diction, you ask? (Well if you didn't you should!) When asking someone to speak clearly most people will say, "Watch your diction," when actually it is the articulation that needs the watching. Let's go back to the dictionary!

Diction means: *"A choice of words or manner of expression."*

Diction refers to *phraseology,* which is the mechanical structuring of sentences or the mode in which they are placed. In plain English:

Diction is: *How you put your sentences together.*

Articulation is: *The manner in which you say them.*

Articulate sounds are the consonants at work, not the vowels. Vowels elongate the sound while the consonants create definition by using the "Tip of the tongue, the lip and the teeth."

Did you ever wonder why operas are performed in Italian, Spanish, Latin, German and very seldom in English? Probably not, but there is a very good reason and it has to do with tongue, lips and teeth. The romance languages use strong tongue, lips and teeth action. That action makes it easier for a singer to sing in the "compressed" mode that is needed to reach those wonderful big, high notes, and still be understood. (A skillful task which by-passes some pop music artists.)

> (♪) *Remember, the vocal cords work like valves and need that powerful compressed air to perform their magic.*

The Italian tongue for example is very energetic, for the consonants are strongly accented and the tip of the tongue is powerful. The tongue rolls and strikes those d's and l's with great strength.

The same is true of the Spanish and German tongues. There is a lot of action going on there. Now think about the English language. Not the Queen's English, because it also uses the tip of the tongue, but our good old lazy tongue American English. We think of a Shakespearean actor as being very articulate and exaggerated, but we certainly can understand all of his words. Now compare that style of acting to some of our American actors. Sometimes it can take a lot of work on our part just to understand what they are saying. If we have to work too hard to understand someone, we quickly lose interest!

As I mentioned before, there are some *regional American accents* that use the tongue more than others. (Nashville and New York for example.) If you combine ethnic language traits with regional accents, you'll find exceptions to all the above rules. Each voice definitely has its own uniqueness, that is what makes the voice so challenging. Anyone who has ever worked with the human voice will definitely agree with that. And speaking of the tongue, here's...

The Tongue
(A Lazy Tongue Creates Lazy Speech!!)

> ♪ *"In the beginning was the WORD", the Bible says, and there definitely had to be a tongue to speak it!*

Scientists agree that one of the most important distinctions between us and the animal is our ability to speak. (Personally, I can think of a few others.)

Ancient fossils show us that 30,000 years ago man's vocal capabilities were in direct correlation to a "hole" called *"The Hypoglossal Canal."* That hole contained the nerves that control the tongue. The bigger the hole the greater the control. (Once again, bigger is better.) Our closest relative, the chimpanzee has a hypoglossal canal half the size of ours.

And speaking of tongue, if you ever looked at a cow's tongue in the meat section of your super market, you would know there is obviously more to a tongue than meets the eye. What you see in your mouth is only the *"tip of the iceberg"* or better still, the *"tip of the tongue."* Many of our major voice problems begin and end with the tongue. Take a look at what lies beneath the surface:

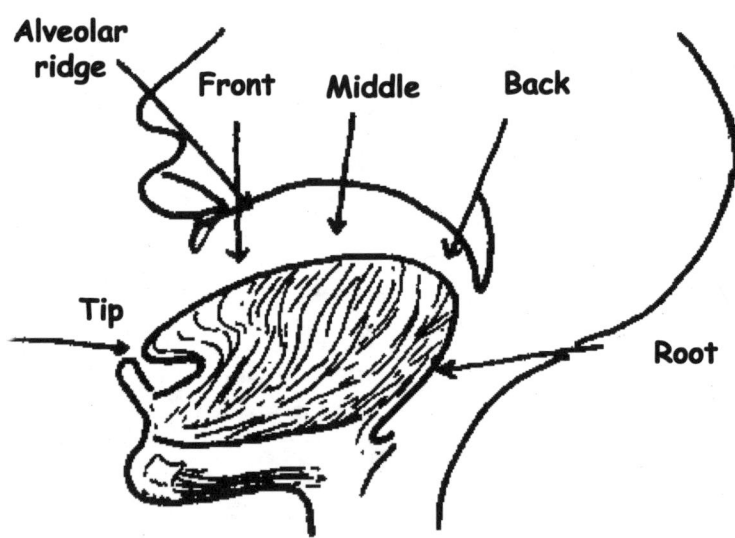

Five Sections of the Tongue

The tongue has always represented speech :

"Hold your tongue."
"Bite your tongue."
"Wag the tongue."
"Couldn't find my tongue."
"Tongue in cheek."
"A good tongue lashing."
"Cat got your tongue."
"Tongue tied."

Two different sets of muscles live together in the tongue: the *constrictor* muscles and the *anti-constrictor* muscles. They can coexist in the same space because each one has a separate job to do and their jobs do not overlap.

These two jobs give the tongue two distinct personalities. The constrictor muscles are the aggressive ones. They snap to *"red alert"* when anything comes into the mouth that even resembles food. They are sensor type muscles much like a spider waiting in the middle of his web for dinner. The slightest movement will set him off running. The constrictor muscles are the "spiders" of our swallow process. When they feel anything enter their space, they are ready to push it to the back of the tongue and swallow it. (Even our words.)

The anti-constrictor muscles are passive. They relax when we yawn. (Are you beginning to get the pattern here?) Once again, the yawn muscles are the good guys when it comes to using the voice.

The aggressive guys, those constrictor muscles, rise up in the back by pulling up the tongue and blocking access to the lower resonators. The pulling back action also drags the voice back to a one o'clock position in the mouth which makes it sound dark and dull. This is where the ability to "dial" the voice forward becomes an all-important skill. (If this is not clear to you, go back to page 76 and do the vocal placement awareness exercise again till you "get it.")

The tip and front of the tongue are directly involved with forming bright sounding words. When the back of the tongue gets involved by raising up the sound is nasal. If the tongue pulls back towards the throat, the sound then becomes dark and covered.

If the tip of the tongue is lazy and weak, the voice is muffled and hard to understand (poor articulation.) There are certain consonants that use the tip of the tongue and keep the voice from pulling back in the throat and becoming muffled. The consonants that keep the swallowed sound out of the voice are formed by placing the tip of the tongue against the ridge behind your top front teeth. They are T, D, N, and L. For the voice to have a bright and articulate sound, the tip of the tongue must be capable of strong powerful consonants. Here is an exercise to "jump start" that lazy tongue.

Tip of the Tongue Exercise:

Run your tongue along the ridge in back of your top teeth. Place the tip in-between your two front teeth. With the tongue in place say TA... DA... NA... LA. Feel the tip of the tongue strike against the ridge to form the consonants. Now using the tip of the tongue like a hammer hitting nails on the ridge, say Ta Ta Ta Ta ... Da Da Da Da ... Na Na Na Na ... La La La La. Do this exercise during the day whenever you can to strengthen the tip of that "lazy" tongue. (Note: Do not involve the jaw, this is a tongue exercise.)

Awareness Exercise:

Listen to the speech patterns of your favorite news anchors, actors and actresses, the people you work with, parents, friends, and all of the voices in your everyday experience... You will be listening for the pronounced D's, L's, N's, and T's. Be aware of the tongue's action and the part it plays in people's vocal sounds, especially their ability to be easily understood by others. (You are studying articulation, not diction.)

Keep your own tongue wide awake and strong when you speak. Then watch how eagerly people will respond when they do not have to work so hard to hear and understand what you are saying.

Lips

The words **"tight lipped"** immediately brings to mind someone who is not willing to share in the conversation. **"Don't give me none 'a your lip,"** is bad english but it alerts us to do verbal battle. **"Zip the lip,"** means "Shhhh." or, "It's a secret." **"Paying lip service,"** brings an image of empty words and meaningless chatter.

 The lips are the gate keepers of our voice.

They can let it out or hold it in. We paint them red to emphasize them and attract attention to them. We pout them when we're unhappy, and we spread them wide in a smile when we are happy. They let everyone know who we are and how we feel. They definitely have a sexual image. They are cosmetic, but they also serve a function in the production of our particular sound.

Relaxed lips form a relaxed pathway for the vocal overtones to come through with the voice sound. Tight lips create a tight sound that does not allow overtones to come through. In the world of articulation, the two lips together are called the bilabial valve, and the sounds that they effect are Ps, B's, M's and W's. Put your two lips together and do this exercise:

Popping the "P's" Exercise:

Begin by gently putting the lips together and allowing each sound to blow through the lips out into the 3rd Dimension of the voice, Length... Start with the P... Pu-Pu-Pu-Pu-Pu. Feel the P pop the lips as it comes through Now, the B... Bu-Bu-Bu-Bu-Bu. Feel it "burble" the lips as it bursts through them. You will notice the P has very little sound while the B bursts forth like an explosion... Time for the W... I think of the W as a wind tunnel for the sound to travel down. Wuh-Wuh-Wuh-Wuh.

Remember to elongate the sound. The lips are gently pursed and relaxed on the W and the mouth is slightly open on the uh. It is vital to always keep the voice moving out of the mouth into the 3rd Dimension, Length. (Remember you can only lengthen the voice using your air.)

Give these lip sentences a try:

P's: Patty's party pleases people.
         Practice Popping "P's" plenty.

B's: Bob's birthday brought big bucks.
         Big brother's been busy.

W's: **Wendy watched Willie's wedding.**
Walking while whistling will ward
off warlocks.

Teeth

Last but not least in this long, but interesting chapter on the voice parts, we come to a subject we can easily "Sink our teeth into," namely, our teeth.

When examining the teeth and their part in the articulation process, they do not "stand alone." They are always paired with something else. Usually it's the lips or the tongue. On their own, besides looking good, the teeth are a slick, hard surface that reflects the sound. Add the lips and the sound changes. To lift the lips (which cushion the sound), off the teeth (which reflect the sound), will automatically produce a brighter sound. In other words, covering the teeth with the lips automatically muffles the bright sound of the voice. People with big teeth need to learn how to control the brightness and people with smaller teeth can add brightness simply by raising the lips off of the teeth.

If the voice has a tendency to be shrill and cutting, try letting the lips relax loosely over the teeth to dampen the sound. If the voice is muffled and hard to distinguish, try showing a bit more teeth and less lip. Remember, sound against a hard surface is more brilliant than sound against a soft surface. Other than that, just be sure to brush and floss regularly and keep 'em happy or better still, just keep 'em. Verbal sounds that are affected by the teeth are:

- **Fu**
- **Vu**
- **Thu**

The *f* and *v* are called labiodental sounds because they involve the lower lip (labio) and the upper teeth (dental). The *th* sound is called linguadental. It involves the tip of the tongue (lingual) peeking through the teeth (dental).

Teeth and Friends Exercises:

Using your basic vowel sounds A-E-I-O-U, put the labiodental (lower lip-upper teeth) and the linguadental (tip of the tongue through the teeth) sounds in front of them as follows:

Labiodental:
Place your upper teeth on your lower lip and say...

> FAY FE FY FO FU
> VAY VE VY VO VU

Linguadental:
Let the tip of your tongue peek through the teeth and say...

> "Th" (as in though.)
> THAY THE THY THO THU
> "Th" (as in that.)
> THAY THE THY THO THU

Now try these sentences:

- **Favorite fantasies feel funny.**
- **Vast vista views vary.**
- **Thirty thousand theatrical themes.**
- **Therefore, they that thither thus, thither themselves.**

Wrapping up the Big One

The "Teeth and Friends" exercise completes the technical part of this owners manual for the human voice. If there is any part of this chapter you did not understand, go back and do the exercises until all of the "voice parts" begin to work together creating the voice of your dreams.

You can look for improvement in the voice as the air learns to flow freely out of the mouth. (Actual voice problems will be covered in detail in the following chapters of this book.) Remember, the *3-Dimensional Voice* method helps the voice become full and powerful, but it must be moving in all three dimensions, **Depth, Width** and **Length**. Be sure you have a basic understanding of the *3-Dimensional* voice process. If you have any questions, write them down on the blank pages of this book entitled "Voice Notes" so you can refer back to them. All questions should all be answered by the time you get to the last page of this book. The question asked the most is:

"How long is it going to take me to learn this stuff?"

Everyone's voice is different and the types of voice problems range from physical to emotional. The study of voice improvement is an "on going" process and just like all functions of the body, you need understanding and constant reminders to keep it in balance. The key to putting all of this information to practice again is understanding. The more you understand and accept the natural process of how the voice works, the faster you can put it into your daily routine. It should be something that delights because you can do such fun and amazing things with your voice.

Speaking of fun, let's all take a trip to the voice store, but first, any questions? Turn the page and write them down so you don't forget them.

♪Voice Notes♪

CHAPTER 4

Browsing Through
The Voice Store

If a thing goes without saying, let it!

Lets go shopping!

What is the Voice Store?

If this is your first visit to the "voice store", you will be amazed at how many types of voices there are. From the good old bargain bins to the top 10 sellers, each voice has a "uniqueness" all its own.

♪   *Think about it...*
How often do you picked up the phone and with just one word, "hello" recognize the voice on the other end?

Voices fit into many categories according to ethnic and regional backgrounds. They also vary according to age and gender. Where we work effects our voice and even how we are educated. Our families effect the type of voice we have, how we phrase our words and the pitch of our tone. Families have definite "traits" that are unique to the family and recognizable to our ears.

Voices are as varied as thumbprints. You can use your voice as identification for credit cards, admittance to top secret buildings and even your computer will recognize you by the sound of your voice. The point here is, the *voice store* is to the voice, what *Amazon and Barns and Nobel.com* are to books! So, where do we start?

As you look over the shelves from the *"Top ten"*, to the *"2 for 1"* bin, it's fun to know there are so many voices to choose from. Better yet, it's great to know you don't have to be stuck your entire lifetime with a voice you don't like!

Let's take a walk through the *"Voice Store"* and try some voices on for size. But before you choose anything, you'll need to do a bit of preparation to help you find the voice image that fits your personality and life-style. **So...**

Ta Da!

It's time to play...

The Matching the Voice Game

The Rules to the Game are as Follows:

• • In column one, you will find a list of voice types.

• • In column two, the names of famous celebrities.

• • Your job, is to match the voices with the celebrities you think they belong to. Remember, hearing is in the *EAR* of the beholder. There are *no right or wrong* answers, there is only your opinion. (Always use a pencil, you may change your opinion.)

Pencils up? Go!

Match The Voices

★Voice Types★

Baby
Whiney
Authorative
Cute
Sexy
New York
Weak
High (Female)
Monotone
English
Deep
Boston
Breathy
Funny
High (Male)
British
Nasal

★Celebraties★

Walter Cronkite
Edith Bunker
Kathleen Turner
James Earl Jones
Willie Nelson
Mary Poppins
Mae West
Betty Boop
Ted Kennedy
Barbra Streisand
Marilyn Monroe
Michael Jackson
Dolly Parton
The Nanny
Bill Clinton
Richard Burton
Sylvester Stallone

Wasn't that fun?

> ♪ *Picking out a new voice to wear is just like picking out a new outfit. Voice styles, like designer fashions, come and go. What's "hot" this year may not be "hot" next year.*

When someone comes along with a certain style, those who aren't happy with their own voices mimic that style. Marilyn Monroe became a popular sex symbol in the 50's and the "in" voice was *soft* and *sexy.* In the early 90's Kathleen Turner's *deep* female voice was often imitated.

Women who want to be taken care of have a tendency to imitate a little girl's baby voice. It keeps people from expecting too much from them. On the other side of that, many men purposely lower their voice to sound like the manly *"voice of authority"* to stay in control.

We are all great imitators. We create what fits the image of who we want to be or who we want people to think we are. We have a voice that we use to talk with children. We have our telephone voice, our talking to the spouse voice, and our at work voice. The interesting thing about all of this is, many of us are not even aware that we are so versatile.

Changing your Voice

Changing your voice will change the way people treat you. That is why it is important to know what kind of a voice you are looking for when you go browsing through the voice store.

If you have a *whiney* voice like the "Nanny," it is hard for anyone to take you seriously, and people often think a female with a low voice is sexy, whether she feels sexy or not.

A baby voice is cute and makes us immediately want to take care of that person. A *deep manly* voice signifies someone we feel will always be there for us in our time of need, like a funeral director. Would you feel as confident and comforted if his voice was thin and high-pitched?

Certain types of voices gravitate toward certain careers. Ten years ago a broadcaster had to have a deep voice so people would listen and believe him when he sold the sponsor's products. Today, sponsors are looking for natural, "real people" sounding voices, or as they say in broadcasting, "Send me a believable voice." If someone auditions with a voice that sounds too much like a broadcaster in today's market, he or she probably would *no*t get the job.

What kind of voice are *YOU* looking for?
Do this exercise to find out:

Voice Awareness Exercise #2

Make every day a day to browse in the voice store. Listen to the voices of people around you and be aware of how they are treated, respected and listened to by others. Give some serious thought to how you would change your own voice. Go back to the voice analysis exam in chapter two. Now that you have a better idea of how the voice actually works, again consider your own voice and how you would change it.

In the privacy of your car, try imitating the voices of commercial actors and radio personalities. Listen to the pitch of the voice and mimic it. Is it low, high, nasal, strained, baby sounding etc. Copy the list of voice types on page 98 and use it as a voice "check list." What type of voice strains your vocal cords and what type of voice makes them feel relaxed? Practice doing the "voices" of other people. You may discover a new "hidden" talent.

Be aware of your own voice patterns. Compare them to the voice patterns of the voices you are imitating. Does your voice change according to who you are talking to? Is your work voice different from your home voice? Try a different voice with your spouse, kids, parents, and even your boss. See if they treat you any different. If you are "soft spoken", try being a bit more aggressive. If you are vocally aggressive, try being a bit more "soft spoken". In other words, practice the fine art of changing you voice to "fit" the occasion just as you would change your attire.

Have fun and be creative!

♪Voice Notes♪

CHAPTER 5

The Mars, Venus Voice Thing

About the only time a woman really succeeds in changing a man is when he's a baby.

When you think male or female, you automatically think *hormones,* those little gems that *keep* us male or female. Like all parts of the human anatomy, the voice is also a gender thing. It's obvious the male and female voices are very different in pitch. There are a few other differences also. Separate corners boys and girls, let's take a peek inside:

THE LADIES ROOM

LADIES ONLY

BUT MEN NEED TO KNOW THIS TOO!

Picture this: (Female version)

Here it is, the most important day of your whole existence! Your new boss has so much faith in you, he has asked you, "Little 'ol you," to give the presentation to an important new client.

You have been preparing a month for this day. Your papers are in order. Your facts are incredible. You've managed to lose those four extra pounds so you can fit into that new mauve suit that's been hanging in your closet all winter. Everything is perfect and then...

You wake up the morning of the big day with hoarseness and vocal fatigue. Not only that, but you can feel your period coming. "Oh no, not today, not PMS."

Has this ever happened to you? All of a sudden, for no reason, a sore, scratchy, hoarse voice rides in from out of nowhere. Is it a cold? Was it the open window you were sitting in front of at the party last Saturday night? Maybe it came from the guy who sneezed yesterday in the elevator. No! No! No, to all three. It's just that little female hormone thing that obviously no one has ever told you about.

We all know premenstrual symptoms bring irritability, headache, bloated feelings, pain in the back, etc. But did you know, PMS also affects the voice? It especially affects us in today's hectic world where most of us over-use and abuse the voice.

To shine some light on the subject, let's go way back to puberty where this whole hormone thing got started:

Just a Kid Again!

Back in junior high while you were busy laughing at all the boys whose voices were bouncing up and down like yo yo's (remember, this is the ladies room), you were probably not aware that you were also going through voice changes of your own.

You always believed the annoying hoarseness that would show up at the worst of times, was caused by yelling too loud at the football game, or maybe laughing too hard with your friends. Or it could be coming from a cold you might be catching. You would always find a reason for the hoarseness even though it seemed to drag on and on and never go completely away.

> (♪) *What you were experiencing was a hormonal reaction to the natural growing process of your voice.*

A woman's larynx is heavily influenced by hormonal changes. These changes take place during puberty, menstruation, pregnancy, and menopause.

With an increase of estrogen, the cartilage and muscles of the larynx enlarge in size. As a woman matures, her vocal cords get longer. *Remember, the longer the cord, the lower the voice.*

While going through puberty and all of its body changes, a young girl can also experience a hoarseness in the voice which causes a "rough edged" sound. She may even feel that "lump in the throat thing." *Not to worry, it's just those vocal cords adjusting to their new size and shape.*

Do be aware that the lump in the throat feeling can sometimes bring about a constant clearing of the voice. This habit can get so bad it follows you into adult life long after the cords have settled and adjusted. The interesting thing is, there was nothing in the throat to clear in the first place. It was only the muscles adjusting to their new position.

As that "little girl" voice becomes the "young lady" voice it can drop in pitch by as much as four musical notes.

(For those of you with no musical background I have included a fun exercise at the end of this chapter to help you understand what a four note drop actually sounds like.)

While a young boy's voice takes a sudden, drastic drop, a young girl going through puberty may experience as many as three smaller voice changes from 11 to 21 years of age. Some women do not have a mature voice until the early twenties. Up until that time, there are periodic bouts with hoarseness and vocal fatigue as those cords grow and adjust. A girl who has no clue to what is going on can get very stressed in times of vocal performance, singing or talking.

I have worked with girls who are ready to give up very successful acting and singing careers for fear their voices would not be able to handle the stress put on them by performing. With an understanding that all of this vocal adjustment is normal and by doing a series of simple exercises to strengthen the voice in its weakened areas the voice returns to normal and the fears vanish. It's amazing what vocal confidence can do for a young, budding career, or for that matter, for any of us!

Time Marches On

After puberty, a woman's voice is still affected by those hormonal changes all of her adult life. She can experience the same hoarseness every month during the PMS days. That's what is happening to our over stressed lady in the beginning of this chapter.

When the emotions take over the body, the body reacts accordingly. We are all aware of the emotional side effects of PMS, but in our culture,(although we joke a lot about PMS,) there is very little understanding of how the voice is affected.

In a study in Paris France by Dr. Jean Abitbol, 22 out of 38 professional female voice users experienced hoarseness and vocal fatigue as a premenstrual symptom. In other studies done, some nasal congestion was also noted. No vocal difficulties were found during ovulation though. Well, at least there's some good news here!

In the world of opera, most contracts with the "Opera Divas" have "Grace days" built into them. This clause assures the diva she will not have to perform during her PMS time of the month. Wouldn't that be nice for the rest of us girls? A few stress free days each month to pamper yourself. What a great concept.

It is good to know that all of those times when you had to speak and thought you were catching a cold, it was just that old PMS messing with your voice. So, put your feet up, throw away those cough drops and reach for a cup of warm herbal (no caffeine) tea to relax those hormonally stressed out cords.

> *(♪)* *It is absolutely VITAL that a woman whose livelihood depends on her vocal abilities, completly understands how important it is to schedule that big presentation before or after PMS days!! Just tell your boss you'd be very happy to meet with the new client but it must be after your "grace days." Yeah right!*

The biggest hormonal "shift" for a woman occurs after menopause. With less estrogen and more testosterone flowing through the body, the membranes covering the vocal cords increase in thickness. This results in a lowering of the vocal pitch. Also, the larynx can drop a bit lower in the neck, again causing a lowering of pitch. As the voice gets heavier, the tendency is to speak slower. (Refer to question #13 on the vocal analysis exam.)

All of these natural events need to be acknowledged, understood and filed away under "things that affect a woman's voice." Then you can go about the task of lifting the voice back to its youthful lightness.

I have worked with many older ladies and never had an experience where the voice was "stuck" in that older woman, heavy, thick voice mode. A more youthful voice is possible. So let's get the "zing" back into the voice! Instead of a face lift, we'll have a "Voice Lift":

Voice Lift Exercise:

Because there are no "levers" to pull and no "buttons" to push that automatically change the voice, you must keep in mind that although each separate part of your vocal mechanism is very efficient at what it does, it does not have a separate brain. You are the "brains" of this outfit. What you think is what you get, so to begin the voice lift process, you must think LIFT. The entire face must think LIFT but, do not lift up the chin, because that will pull the larynx out of position. (You knew that, right?)

It is best to do this exercise in a completely relaxed state of being and to achieve this...

Let's Try a Bit of Self-hypnosis:

In self- hypnosis when you want to send signals to the body, the process is started by closing the eyes and going into a completely relaxed state of consciousness as follows;

1. Close your eyes and relax your face... begin counting backwards from 10 very slowly... 9 ... feel your mouth begin to relax... now count 8... relax the lips, allowing them to feel heavy... 7... the tongue is relaxed, completely relaxed as if in a yawn position... 6 ... the jaw is dropped and very relaxed. All the jaw tension is released... 5 ...the tightness and tension between the eyes is now completely relaxed... 4 ... the eyes are closed and the eyelids are relaxed... 3 ... the forehead feels relaxed. All the tightness and tension are completely gone ... 2 ... the top of your head is now relaxed and open for instruction ...1 ... the entire head area from the neck up is one completely relaxed unit... In that relaxed state with your lips closed, picture the biggest smile you can smile lifting your entire face to fit into it... Now think of the Joker from Batman, with a painted mouth all the way up to his ears.

If you have any problem visualizing that image, take a look:

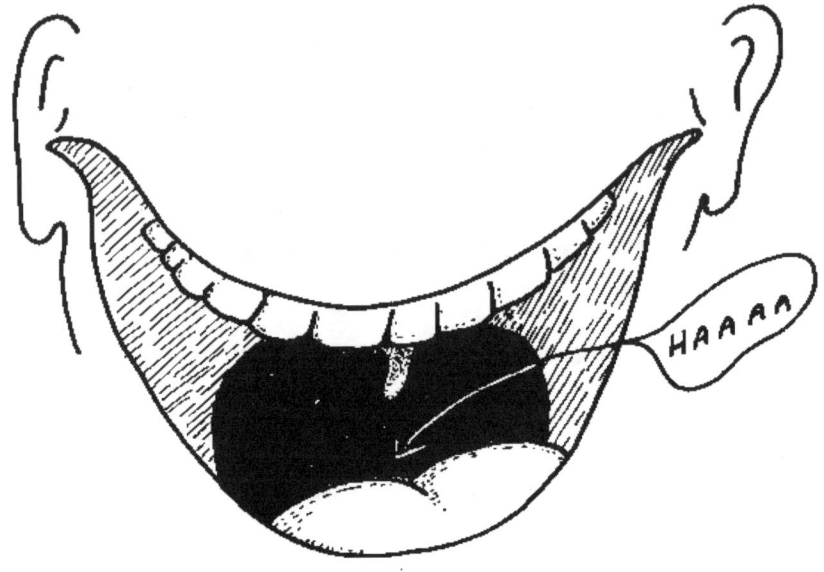

Open your mouth. Now lift it and shape it to fit inside of that painted smile. Feel the entire mouth, soft palette, hard palette, uvula and teeth all lifted to fit that smile... While in that relaxed lifted smile position say "Haaaa".... say "Hi, how are you." Say "Hi, my name is_____". Talk to all of the voice parts and tell them how light and free they feel, "My tongue is light and free." "My jaw is dropped and free," etc. Remember, the parts have no brain, they will believe what you believe. Believe in your new lifted voice. It works!

It's time to take a trip to the men's room...

THE MALE VOICE

Ask a man, "What are the most important qualities you want in your voice?" 9 out of 10 will answer, "My voice needs to sound more manly and authoritative so people will listen to what I have to say." They also desire strength and power. These are all words that define a "man's man," someone who is respected and listened to. I don't hear the words gentle, soft, or warm very often, although *these* are the qualities *women* love in a man's voice. (Hint, hint.)

Just as they affect a woman's voice, hormones also affect a man's voice. Every man can go back to the eighth grade and remember when he went from sounding like a girl, passed through the dreaded cracking stage, and finally settled into that manly lower voice. (Preferably before he entered high school.)

In the section on vocal cords, you learned it's the length of the cord that determines how deep the voice can go. The longer the cord, the deeper the voice.

A young male's vocal cords are the same size as a female's. When that good old "burst" of testosterone hits, *it affects the cords and the larynx big time.* The cords lengthen by approximately ten millimeters, give or take a millimeter. This increase in cord size also affects the larynx. It becomes obvious when it pokes out from the throat. This "poking out thing" is affectionately called *The Adam's Apple.*

The male voice can drop in pitch by as much as an octave. One octave is a musical term for a block of 8 notes, going from ABCDEFG and back to A. You can start with any letter (note) and come back to the one you started with like FGABCDE and back to F, etc. This is called a scale. Reminder: There is a fun exercise in the back of this chapter for anyone who is interested in the degrees a voice can rise up or drop down.

Is There Vocal Life After Puberty?

After the puberty stage, a man's voice will stay relatively steady until his later years when the testosterone levels go back down. This causes the voice to thin and the pitch to rise back up again.

This information is in all the medical books I've read on the voice. In my experience working with older men, I have found the voice to be capable of lowering back down with the right exercise and an understanding of what is physically happening. Instead of weakening, the voice can actually get stronger. Most of the weakness, regardless of testosterone, is from improper use and vocal abuse. (More on this in a later chapter.)

Since the length of the cord affects the tone or pitch of the voice and men have a need for the deep manly sound, the question is, can a man who is born with a shorter cord than say, James Earl Jones, find a way to lower his voice, or is he destined to be a tenor all his life? The answer is yes and no. Yes, there is a way to lower the voice and no, he does not have to remain a tenor in a baritone work place.

> ♪ *Many a career in the man's world depends on the authority of his vocal image.*

A large "in charge kind of guy" with a high pitched thin voice has difficulty competing in the corporate world because of his vocal image, especially if most of his work is done by telephone. A lawyer with a high- pitched voice has a harder time convincing a jury he speaks the truth.

I don't believe anyone was ever sued because of voice discrimination, but surveys and polls show us to be *very influenced* by a man voice. (This can apply to women also but this is the men's room.)

One Gallop poll showed that we like to listen to Bill Cosby more than any other celebrity, followed by Dan Rather. The celebrity whose voice was rated the lowest was Sylvester Stallone. (Yo, Adrian.) He has a mumbling, monotone drone which makes it hard to understand his words, however his natural speaking voice is much clearer than the characters he plays.

The "Manly" Sound

In searching for a "manly" sound, many a man has tried to speak in a forced lower voice at his work place only to find that by the end of the day his voice has become a hoarse whisper.

The method used by most men to lower the voice is to drop down on the vocal cords with weight. A few hours of constant pounding on the cords and they just say **No! No more pounding. No more sound. No more voice.** Give the vocal cords a day of rest and they bounce right back. But if weight is put on them day after day, the end result is chronic dysphonia. (A medical term for poor voice quality. See; *When to Take Your Voice to a Doctor*, chapter nine.)

This causes those airy, breathy tones that bring to mind Bill Clinton during his campaign for President or Pete Wilson, (who was Governor of California and also a Presidential candidate).

Both men had higher pitched, soft, natural voices, but when campaigning they tried to speak in a louder, lowered voice to show more authority so the American people would trust and believe them. (It's that lower voice image thing you guys have to live with.) The end result was, Pete developed nodules on his vocal cords from constantly abusing his voice and ended up in surgery. He completely lost the ability to use his voice and dropped out of the race for president. Bill won the presidency, but had voice problems all of his term. (Yeah I know! But this is a book about voice.)

It was a bad political year for voices, but a very lucrative year for speech therapists. All of this brings us to that most perplexing problem you guys have to deal with:

Improving Your "Manly" Image

Lawyer, teacher, sportscaster, actor, news anchor, president (of anything), pastor, even the local lounge lizard; a man needs that wonderful voice that melts the hearts of women and makes all men respect and admire him.

If you are one of those lucky guys born with long, strong vocal cords, you can go to the next chapter. (Unless of course your best buddy is one of those "short cord guys," then you can read on and help him to change his entire existence. He will owe you big time for that.)

> ♪ *Understanding you can get the lower voice sound you want by increasing the resonance, not pushing the volume button, brings us back once again to the 3-Dimension's of the Voice: Depth, Width and Length.*

In chapter three, you learned to not add weight to the vocal cords to lower the pitch. It is vital to stay completely away from the vocal cord area.

To increase the lower tones of the voice, you must drop the voice all the way down into the 1st-Dimension of the voice, *Depth*, filling the entire rib cage with full, vibrating sound. The following exercise will show you how to do it.

Manly Awareness Exercise:

Put your finger on the abdominal diaphragm (you know the spot.) Open the mouth in that familiar yawn position and laugh like Santa, "Ho, ho, ho." Feel the now familiar "jumping" of the abdominal diaphragm as it pumps the air and vibrates the chest with sound..Remember, the sound is traveling up from the 1st Dimension, Depth, and out of the mouth to the 3rd Dimension, Length...

Keeping the finger on the diaphragm, in yawn position manually push the air out while saying ..."Haaa... Haaaa... Haaal... Haaart... Haaarms... Home... Heed." Do not allow a "glottal attack" (a harsh striking sound in the cords) to occur on the Ahhhhh. Say it gently on the breath.

The "Bullwinkle" Exercise:

Now, while you are in the lower resonance yawn position, say "BO... BO... BO," allowing the jaw to drop and the lips to "burble" so the "BO" pops out of the mouth through the lips

This is called a "Bullwinkle the Moose" exercise, as in "Rocky and Bullwinkle," because when you begin talking in that lower yawn position, you'll sound just like Bullwinkle. Try it, say "Oh hello Rocky" in your "Bullwinkle" voice. (It also sounds a bit like Barney Rubble of the Flintstones.)

With practice you can become a master of the lower resonance *"yawn voice"*. Use it when you need a more manly sound. (You can also astound your friends at parties with your impersonations of Bullwinkle and Barney Rubble.)

There is one more "Lower Voice Exercise" I would like you to do:

Go right now and get a tape recorder... I'll wait. Have you got it? Record yourself reading any article from the newspaper. Do you have a newspaper handy? ... I'll wait. Now, Play it back and ask yourself these questions :

_____ *Is your voice monotone like Sylvester Stallone's?*

_____ *Is it filled with too many high tones and very few low tones?*

_____ *Does it sound "stuck" in the back of your throat?*
_____ *Does it sound like you have a cold because it sits right in your nose?*
_____ *Is it dark and dull?*
_____ *Do you mumble?*

Try reading the article again in your "Bullwinkle" lower voice. Don't forget to record yourself so you can give a listen...

If your voice still sounds monotone and lifeless, try talking with a little more up and down inflection to add some interest. Practice the following questions raising and lowering the pitch on each word as shown:

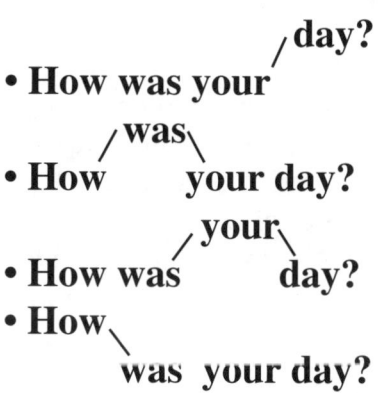

- **How was your** /**day?**

- **How** /**was**\ **your day?**

- **How was** /**your**\ **day?**

- **How**\ **was your day?**

♪ VOCAL VARIETY IS THE SPICE OF LIFE!

Lower Voice Awareness Exercise:

Study the male newscasters on all major TV networks. Listen to the easy relaxed lower tones of their voices and the inflection as the voice glides up and down in pitch when they are speaking. This "gliding" up and down adds the emotion to their news copy. Without it, they wound sound monotone and boring. Practice the "glide" technique as you read the morning paper. Become your own "newsman."

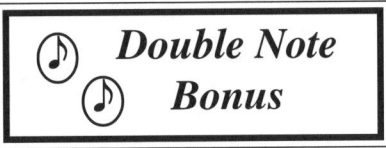

Musical Awareness Exercise:

In *Ladies Only* and *The Men's Room*, references to the voice dropping in pitch at puberty were made. (A four note drop for a female and an eight note drop in pitch for a male.) I stated in both chapters there would be an exercise for the "musically impaired" to show you just what a four note drop and an octave (eight note) drop in a voice sounds like, well, get your pitch pipes ready 'cuz here we go!

Did you see Julie Andrews in "The Sound Of Music?" If you didn't see it, rent it and watch it before you do this exercise.

Can you just see her twirling through the hills? Cut to the scene where she is teaching the kids to sing. You are now one of the kids and Julie is now your music teacher...

The song she is going to teach you is "Doe Re Mi". Do, Re, Mi is the beginning of a classic vocal exercise called Solfeggio. In this lesson, instead of moving up the musical scale with letters of the alphabet, ABCDEFG, Solfeggio takes you up the scale using consonants with vowel sounds. These sounds are Do, Re, Mi, Fa, So, La, Ti, Do.

Like all good teachers, Julie has her own way of teaching the scale to "you" kids. She says: "Doe, Ray, Me, Far, Sew, La, Tea, and back to Doe." (It sounds about the same with just a few minor adjustments.)

Ready?

Hold it! Before we start let's open up those vocal pipes: Me-Me-Me, La-La-La, Lo-Lo-Lo, Lu-Lu, Lu. (This of course is not a serious vocal warm up for all of you serious voice people and this exercise is not to show the world what a great singer you are but it will help you to feel the degrees that the voice drops in pitch at puberty. For all of you die-hard vocalist, read my book *The 3-Dimensional Singers Voice.*) Oh... If you can't remember the melody to this song and didn't have time to rent the video, just ask your kids to join you, they will know it.

OK. Let's sing!

Doe Re Mi

Maria: (Speaks to the children*)*
"I am going to teach you how to sing.

(She sings)
Let's start at the very beginning
A very good place to start.
When you read you begin with ...

Kids:
A B C

Maria:
When you sing, you begin with Doe Re Mi.

Kids:
Doe Re Mi.

Maria:
Doe Re Mi... The first three notes just
happen to be, Doe Re Mi...

Kids:
Doe Re Mi

Maria:
Doe Re Mi Fa So La Ti...
(Spoken)
Come on, I'll make it easy for you.
Listen...

Maria sings:

Doe, a deer, a female deer
Ray, a drop of golden sun
Me, a name I call myself
Far, a long way to run
Sew, a needle pulling thread
La, a note to follow sew
Tea, a drink with jam and bread
That will bring you back to
Doe, oh, oh...

All together now, one more time from the top...

Doe, a deer, a female deer
Ray, a drop of golden sun
Me, a name, I call myself
Far, a long, long way to run
Sew, a needle pulling thread
La, a note to follow sew
Tea, a drink with jam and bread
That will bring you back to Doe.
                              The End.

Give Yourselves a Big Hand!

Now that your spirits are lifted and you can sing **Doe, Re, Mi, Fa, Sol, La, Ti, Doe** with the best of them, let's hear what a voice-drop sounds like. To do this, we will first accend *up* the scale starting with Doe at the bottom.

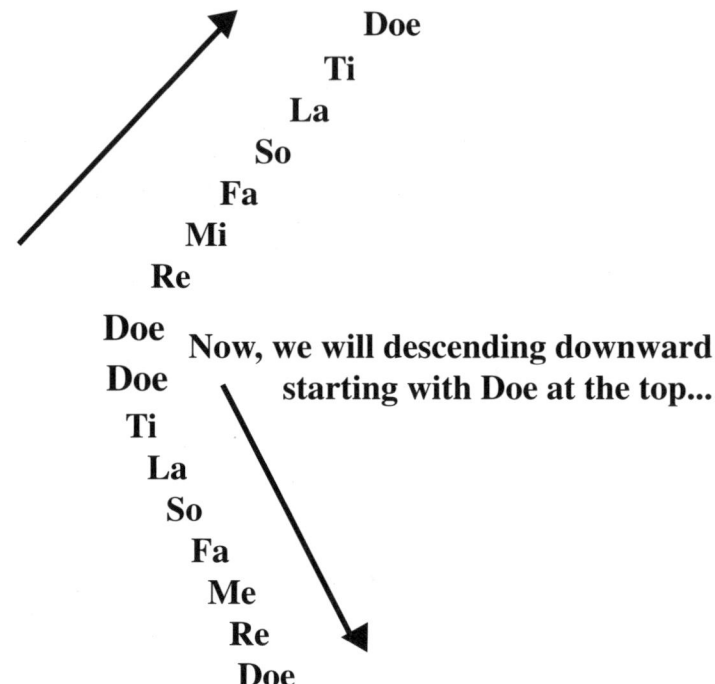

Doe
Ti
La
So
Fa
Mi
Re
Doe

Doe Now, we will descending downward
Ti starting with Doe at the top...
La
So
Fa
Me
Re
Doe

This is an octave (8 notes) drop in pitch for you guys, and a four note drop for you girls.

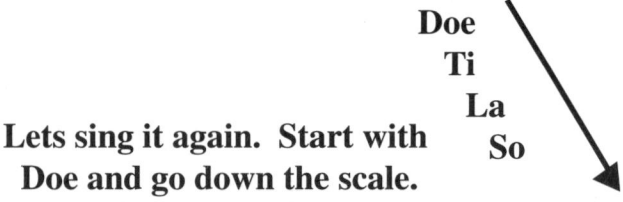

Doe
Ti
La
Lets sing it again. Start with **So**
Doe and go down the scale.

Wasn't that informative and fun?

CHAPTER 6

Emotions And Other Fearful Things

People are like teabags... They don't know their own strength until they get into hot water.

No where in the human body does the affect of our emotional temperature show up faster then in our voice.

Sometimes it comes as an "un-budging lump" (*larynx up*) in the throat that no amount of annoying clearing can force out. Sometimes it results in the pitch of the voice rising so high, you feel like "Mickey Mouse" in a suit. Sometimes the mouth gets so dry the voice sounds like scratchy sand paper. Sometimes the voice is so shaky you sound like you're standing on a ski slope with a wind chill factor of 65 degrees below zero, and sometimes it just feels like two invisible hands are choking the words right out of you.

You are Having an Emotional, Vocal Stress Attack!

The smallest change in our emotions creates an instant reaction in our vocal mechanism. In today's stress filled world, as our emotions go up and down, so does our voice. Under stress, and even under excitement, the voice will tense up and feel tight and constricted. The pitch will automatically go up, and sometimes (like the man in chapter one), the voice will just "cut out" completely.

Whether we are auditioning for a play, taking an oral exam, singing a song at the Grammy's, or firing an employee, we have all felt the dreaded *vocal stress*. If you are like me, **YOU HATE IT!** I have ignored many opportunities that came my way simply to avoid being put in the same room with "Mr. Stress." (I'm a total stress chicken.)

We try to make excuses by saying, "Please excuse me, I'm just a little nervous." But nervousness is not the cause; nervousness is the effect. Before this gets too complicated, let's define the word *stress* so we can understand this culprit.

Stress, the word, was popularized in 1974 by Hans Selyer in his classic book *Stress without Distress*. After years of studying the effects of stress in his laboratory in Vienna, Dr. Selyer came to the conclusion that:

> (♪) *"Stress is the non specific response of the body to any demand made upon it." In other words, stress is an over-stimulation of the body.*

Over-stimulation comes from both unpleasant and pleasant situations. The problem with the voice is that it doesn't know the difference. Feeling very happy at your daughter's wedding can cause as much vocal stress as feeling sadness at someone's funeral. (I've had to sing at both, and my voice did *not* know the difference.)

It is simply an uncomfortable demand on the body to do something out of its "comfort zone." This results in a negative body reaction . As with many responses in our bodies, our stress reactors come in different degrees. In responding to the same event, you may be completely stressed out while it wouldn't bother me at all. We now know the effects of stress on the *whole body* can be life threatening, but in this book we are only concerned how it affects the vocal parts. Its effects are not *life threatening* to the voice, but it sure can "squeeze the life" right out of it.

> (♪) *Statistically, about two-thirds of all voice disoders treated in vocal clinics have no organic cause. **

*Statistical quote by Danial R. Boone Ph.D., Professor of speech at The University of Arizona, Tuson, Arizona

These emotions have major effects on the human voice system:

- Disappointment
- Frustration
- Happiness
- Sadness
- Sympathy
- Disgust
- Anger
- Fear
- Doubt
- Love
- Hate

How they can affect the voice:

- Raised pitch
- Shortness of breath
- Harshness
- Feeling of tightness
- Choking feeling
- Constant throat clearing
- Nervous shaking
- Pain in throat area
- "Yodel" effect (Pitch break)

- **Monotone (one level pitch)**
- **Breathy sound**
- **Weakness**
- **Too loud**
- **No voice at all**
- **Hoarseness**

How they can affect the body:

- **Dry mouth**
- **Dizziness (light headed)**
- **Nausea**
- **Weak (No energy)**

> ♪ *Of course, the best way to eliminate the effects of stress in the voice and body is to eliminate the cause of the stress!*

Be it money, job, relationships or simply a lack of self worth, whatever or whomever is causing the stress problem, it's best to remove that if it damages the voice.

This is easier said than done of course, unless you can relocate to an island in the Pacific, and even way out there, you'd probably find some reason to stress. It looks like stress is here to stay. What that means to the voice is, we must find ways to keep it from ruining our **"Kodak Moments."**

Understanding the problems will help to lighten the *stress load* on the voice, so I'll take the effects of stress just listed and address them one at a time:

Raised Pitch:

When we get nervous, our voice begins to go up like a stress meter. You can bet it's that larynx on the rise. We have done exercises in previous chapters to help lower the larynx and dip the voice down into its 1st Dimension, *Depth*. Yawning the larynx back into dropped position will also help adjust the pitch. Think of the "Bullwinkle" (Bo, Bo, Bo) exercise on page 116.

Sipping water also helps to get the larynx down and out of *swallow position*. By simply completing the swallowing process the larynx will sit back down in its relaxed position. Always be sure the chin is down and not pulling the neck up.

Shortness of Breath:

Shortness of breath will make us feel like we are hyper-ventilating. We tend to breathe with the top part of the lungs, filling the small upper portion with air instead of filling the larger bottom portion of the lungs. Take a relaxed moment to focus your breath back to the bottom of the lungs. Let the diaphragm breathe for you the way you learned to breathe in chapter three. Do not hold your breath or try to speak long sentences without breathing. This will only make you gasp for the breath. Breathe more often when you talk. It will also help you to speak slower.

Harshness:

Harshness is caused by tension and also by the voice sitting too low on the vocal cord. This action results in a scraping, glottal sound, much like a squeaking door (eeeeeeeeeeeeek). It is very irritating to sit in an audience and listen to someone who does this for an extended period of time. Please give your friends the right to tell you if you sound like this. If you don't feel comfortable doing that, tape record yourself and just listen. **You'll hear it!** People who have this habit very seldom hear it when they are speaking and they refuse to listen to their own voice played back on tape. The best way to fix this annoying sound, is to lift the voice off of the vocal cords and raise up the pitch by one note. Remember our song Do, Re Me? Start with doe and go up one note to Re:

Now speak at the level you landed on with the "Re" tone. That should fix the problem. It will sound higher in your ear, but believe me the rest of us will not even notice the difference.

Tightness:

Tightness is usually centered in that *"wild jaw"* we did battle with back in chapter three. When we get nervous the jaw has the tendency to grip and grind our teeth, causing tightness in the voice. The solution; open your mouth and relax the jaw, then do the "yawn sigh" a few times. One of my incredible teachers, Roland Wyatt, once told me to "chew" the days of the week to relax the jaw, so start chewing while saying Monday, keep chewing Tuesday, Wednesday, etc. By the time you get to Sunday, the jaw is nice and relaxed.

Choking Feeling:

This is again caused by the nervous, raised larynx. It feels like the "Grippers" have us by the throat and we can't swallow. It can be a moment of sheer terror when we are in front of an audience and our swallower "freezes". Again, the best way to relieve that feeling is to sip water and "jump start" the swallowing process.

> ♪ *Always, always keep your water handy, especially if you have a tendency to be nervous.*

Clearing the Throat:

This is a very common problem for speakers. We have all had to sit in the audience while the speaker constantly cleared his (or her) throat. It not only irritates the audience but it is extremely irritating to the vocal cords of the speaker.

As stated in a previous chapter, this can be a nervous habit carried over from puberty. The mucous that coats the vocal cords is there to protect them (remember, the vocal cords are mucous membranes), and when someone continually scrapes out the mucous to clear the throat, the body's defense system calls up the "Mucous Army" to protect the cords.

Here Comes the Mucous Army.

I love these guys!

> ♪ *The more we clear the mucous, the bigger the army gets. You can see what a useless exercise clearing the throat is!*

If the mucous army begins to resemble *The Gulf War,* go into yawn position with a dropped, relaxed jaw, put your finger on your abdominal diaphragm, and manually push the air up and out of the mouth while saying "hut... hut... hut."

You will feel the breath explode through the *underside* of the vocal cords, clearing the debris along the way. The cords create the sound which moves up and out of the mouth on the breath and projects into the 3rd Dimension, **Length.**

Nervous Shaking:

Not only do your knees and your hands shake, but the part you can't hide when you really get nervous is the one that shakes the worst, **your voice.** In singing, we call it vibrato when the voice oscillates up and down. In speaking we call it embarrassing.

When the whole body is shaking with nervous energy, the voice is going to go along with the crowd. Your best defense is to know your presentation material well, and to have good notes. Practice in front of a mirror and eliminate as many things as you can that could go wrong.

If possible, during your presentation stand in back of the podium, this gives you something to hang on to and you will feel safer than just standing out in front of the people. Speak slowly. Shaky, rapid speech is impossible to understand. I can assure you, as you "meet your speech lion," the task will get easier. If it doesn't and you are completely panicked, visit your local hypnotherapist. I've seen wonders occur in a couple of sessions.

The "Yodel" Effect:
(Those pesky pitch breaks)

Like a chain with a weak link, the voice also has certain areas in the pitch levels that tend to be weaker than others. The voice travels up and down in pitch when we talk, and when we hit one of those weak areas, the voice "yodels" over it. Young boys experience this during puberty (as mentioned in the last chapter). In the world of operatic vocal training, when the voice breaks it is called a "wolf tone" because the voice resembles a howling wolf. (Try it. When you get really good at wolf tones, you can graduate to the "Tarzan yell".)

To completely avoid those pitch break areas is impossible, especially when the voice becomes excited. (Unless you speak in a monotone voice.) We must become aware of where they are in the voice chain and add support to the note. Think of those lottery balls spinning on top of that column of air. If you shut down the air that supports them, they will tumble and scatter. If you keep them supported with the air, they will spin on and on. When you hit one of those pitch break areas, send it more supporting air by pushing down on the pelvic diaphragm (the compressor).

Another solution would be to raise the voice up a tone or lower it down a tone depending on where the break lies in your own voice. (Back to the hills with Julie and Doe, Ray, Me.)

Monotone: (One level speech)

To understand what monotone is, simply talk on one pitch level with no fluctuation at all. You'll sound like a robot or an AT&T operator. Now that's monotone! It's called, *single unvaried key pitch*. Sing "Doe" and talk only on that pitch. It's *BORING*. That's what monotone is...boring! So, if you find your self boring when you listen to Your voice on the tape recorder, here's what you can do; Go to your nearest bookstore and buy a book called *Talk to Win* by Lillian Glass, Ph.D. Dr. Glass has worked with many of Hollywood's finest and her exercises are wonderful, especially the ones to raise and lower the voice pitch. In the meantime, here is an easy exercise to try:

"Up -Down Glide Exercise:

Say the word "Ah" and slide up a scale for two notes (Doe to Re... one note. Re to Mi = two notes), holding each note for three seconds. (Doe...Re...Mi..) Now use "Ah," ready?

Ah (Mi)
Ah (Re)
Ah (Doe)

(I am using the Doe, Re, Mi so you can get your correct pitch. Now... aren't you glad you learned that song? Back to the exercise...)

Don't strain your voice. Make sure it feels comfortable to you as you slide up and down the scale. Slide the "Ah" vowel down the scale for two notes starting with Mi to Re to Doe. Hold each note for three seconds.

Ah (Mi)
Ah (Re)
Ah (Doe)

Now glide up the scale and back down on an "Ah" in one breath...

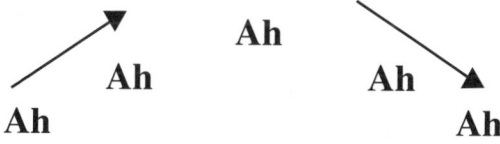

We will now use sentences instead of the "Ah" but stay with your three notes both up and down.

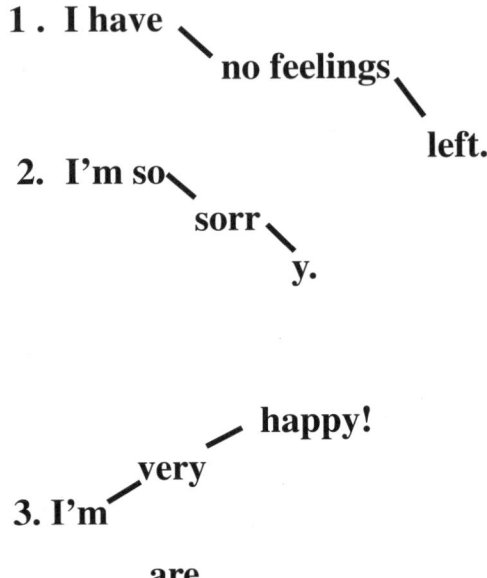

1 . I have
    no feelings
        left.

2. I'm so
    sorr
      y.

       happy!
     very
3. I'm

    are
4 How   you today?

Try these *pitch changing* **sentences,** then make up some of your own. You will find when you raise and lower the pitch in the middle of your words it will make them sound more natural. If you constantly pull up the end of your word, that tends to make everything a question. If you drop the end of the word, that makes it a statement!

Pitch Awareness Exercise:

Listen to the pitch patterns of those around you. Take note of what voices please you and what voices do not. Instead of dwelling on what is wrong with a voice, concentrate on what is right. Try imitating the voice sounds that you do like. Notice also if the ends of sentences go up (question?), or down (statement!). Watch out for that in your own voice. This is an awareness exercise... Be aware!

Breathy Sound:

A breathy voice is a signal the cords are not coming together and air is leaking through them. When we get hoarse, for whatever reason sickness or voice abuse, the first sign something is wrong is breathiness in the voice.

The breathier the voice, the softer and weaker it feels. A soft, breathy voice is considered feminine and sexy for a woman. Marilyn Monroe was the female symbol of the breathy voice. Many male rock singers have that raspy, breathy quality that sounds great in a recording studio but does not hold up well under the rigors of a concert tour. Then again, some people are just born with vocal cords that have a natural "air leak" in them. This leaking air will even give kids a rough gravely voice. (Froggy in The Little Rascals had one of those cute, raspy, kid voices.).

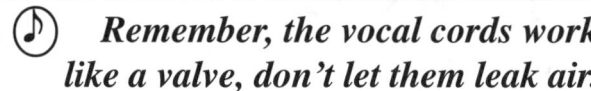

> ♪ *Remember, the vocal cords work like a valve, don't let them leak air.*

When you have a leak in your valve, you lose compression. When you lose compression, you lose strength and power in your engine. And so it is with the voice. (Review chapter three, *The Vocal Cords.*)

There *is* something we can do to strengthen the cords when they "leak." It is a matter of mentally focusing on them. Because we cannot reach them physically to tighten them we must send them a mental picture of what we are asking for. We need to create tension in the cords so they will become as taut as a well-tuned guitar string. When the vocal cords have the correct *tension,* the tone is crisp, and the air will come through them in a powerful, thin stream. If we can keep the hole in the cord the air comes through small enough, the air will not leak. This is done by pushing down on the pelvic diaphragm and mentally visualizing the cords squeezed in.

Study this illustration of the vocal cords so you can picture in your mind the area that needs to be squeezed and tightened.

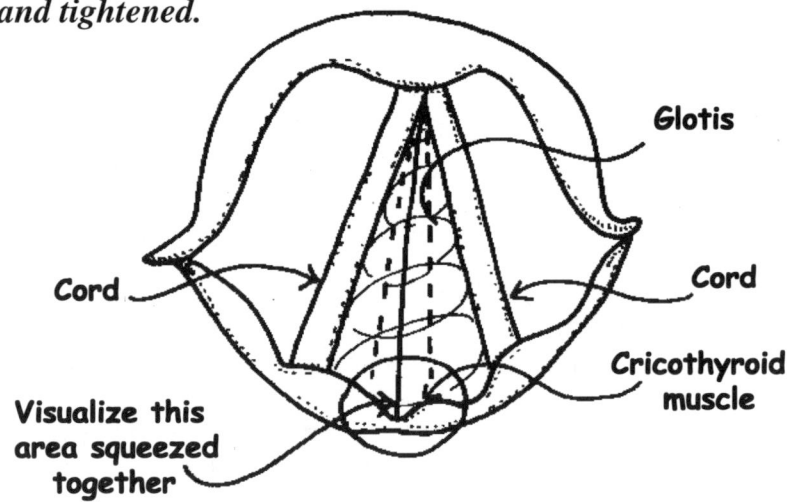

Glotis

Cord

Cord

Cricothyroid
muscle

Visualize this
area squeezed
together

The Vocal Cords

The pelvic diaphragm is the compressor. Pushing down on the base of the rectal area begins the process (as stated in chapter three, *The Pelvic Diaphragm*). Think of mentally placing the sound between your index finger and your thumb and squeezing it tightly while pushing on the pelvic diaphragm. Now speak a whole sentence while holding your finger and thumb together and compressing your sound. Practice this, so at your will, and when it is needed, you can activate the compressor. Train those vocal cords to come in and tighten at your command.

Vocal Weakness:

A weak voice can be caused by leaks in the cords, a lack of support, inadequate air supply, PMS, physical illness in the body, even a lack of energy and drive.

> ♪ *A weak voice is only an effect. You must find the cause before you can fix it!*

It has been my experience, when *all* other physical causes have been eliminated, a weak voice comes from a simple lack of self worth. In other words, the less sure we feel about our vocal contributions, the softer and weaker we tend to speak. We secretly hope no one will hear us because what we have to say is of no importance anyway. Women tend to fall into this vocal trap more often than men do.

This may begin to resemble *arm chair* psychology, but through the years, as my soft voiced clients began to understand and use their vocal abilities, they gained confidence and energy in their presentations and communications. The automatic result of their new self confidence was a greater strength in the speaking voice.

Loud Voice:

First, have your ears check to make sure your hearing is not the problem. Then be aware of the volume levels of those around you and adjust your own volume to match. *It is vital that you learn to listen to others and simply SPEAK SOFTER!* (More on this in the next chapter *The Voice and the Telephone.*)

Hoarseness, and Pain:

These two symptoms have many causes and again, they are the effect of something not right in the voice, not the cause. They will be covered in chapter nine, *When to Take Your Voice to a Doctor.*

Dry Mouth:

This is my favorite problem to solve and it is worth the entire price of this book to anyone who speaks for a living. Dry mouth is mainly the result of nervousness and stress. The only exterior causes I have found are the dehydrating effects of air-conditioning, anything containing caffeine or alcohol, decongestants that dry up the mucous (they tend to dry up the saliva as well), and certain prescription drugs. If you're giving that all important presentation and must take any prescription drug, check with your doctor for side effects like dehydration from decongestants, or anything that could possibly affect the voice.

So there you are up in front of the group again...

You have forgotten your glass of water, the one that should always be sitting right next to your notes. You can't interrupt your talk because your audience is "all ears!" and waiting for your answer to the big problem. Your mouth feels like the Mojave Desert is alive and well inside of it. What do you do?

Here is a 3 Note Tip!!!!

Take a dramatic pause and bite down on the tip of your tongue. Of course, do it so no one knows what you are doing. (It's just our little secret.) You can even smile while you do this. The salivary glands think you are going to eat and they flood your mouth with that much needed elixir of the vocal cords, saliva. Ahhhhh!

STAGE FRIGHT

Just to hear those two words brings terror to the heart, sweat to the brow, and a quiver to the voice.

All of us at some time in our life have had to stand before a group of our peers with our knees knocking and butterflies dancing in our stomach. As our shaky hands held our speech and our dry mouth tried to spit out the words, we prayed to a merciful God that we would not throw up or pass out in front of all these people.

Those my dear, dear friend are classic symptoms of stage fright!

There is no magic formula to abolish stage fright. Many books have been written suggesting everything from going back to your inner child, to taking a good stiff drink. It's no light, laughing matter to those who have a severe stage fright problem. Many a career has been cut short because of the serious effects of stage fright.

The Stage Fright Monster

Those of you who are natural "hams" and can hardly wait to hit the stage can skip this section. For the rest of us, the best solution to the problem is to face *"The Stage Fright Monster"* as often as we can. Instead of avoiding situations where you have to talk, seek them out. Speak to anyone, anywhere. Join a local Toastmasters group where it's safe and speak, speak, speak.

Use the relaxing techniques in this book, or take a yoga class and learn to calm yourself. Meditation techniques are good to do before any big event and remember, for those severe cases where nothing else works, hypnosis has come to the rescue more than once. (More on hypnosis later in this section.)

Stage fright is a mental cause with extreme physical effects. The good news is, it can be conquered!

Be well prepared!!!

One way I have found to combat stage fright is to know my material inside and out. The more secure I am in my material the less margin there is for error. I've said that before, but it is well worth repeating here! I rehearse each presentation faithfully, even if I've done it many times before.

Before we leave the subject of stage fright I'd like to share a personal experience I had with hypnosis that made me a total believer.

Scary "Stuff"

I was playing a lead in the musical *42nd Street*. In one of the musical numbers, I had to be hoisted up while sitting in a swing 20 feet in the air, all the way to the rafters. If that wasn't frightening enough, I had to sit up there through six minutes of a dance number before they lowered me back down center stage. Sitting up there while my brain imagined everything that could possibly go wrong, I would panic. I had a choice, I could refuse to do it, which would ruin the end of the number, or find a way to sit there and not be afraid that I would faint, fall out of the swing and end up a big "splat" on the stage.

Enter the hypnotherapist: After one session (which was extremely interesting), I was able to sit up there without panicking throughout 12 performances. I just sat up there while the words, *"Forget Your Troubles, C'mon Get Happy"* sang through my brain, blocking out all my fears.

It worked!

I can't say I was *not* relieved on closing night knowing that was the last time I'd be sitting up there, but I got through it, and I didn't faint and end up "flattened"! Even now, with that song programmed in my head as a brain blocker, whenever I get into a situation I have trouble handling, I just open my mouth and sing...

♪   ♪   ♪
"Forget you're troubles com'on
♪ get happy..." ♪

...and I am ready to face my lions. (It even works in the dentist chair.) Psychologists say we do not come into this world with stage fright, it is something we learn when we get here. If we can learn it, we can certainly unlearn it.

A review of 8 easy voice techniques to help you relax before your big presentation.

---

1. **The good old "yawn sigh" to relax the jaw and open the throat.**

2 **The "pant breath" exercise to activate the abdominal diaphragm and send those "cleansing puffs" of air up through the under side of the cords.**

3. **Tongue and lip rolls to loosen the tension in those areas.**

4. **Biting the tip of the tongue to send that glorious moisture (saliva) to your dry cords.**

5. Chewing the days of the week to
   relax the jaw.

6. Taking a slow relaxing breath from the
   abdominal diaphragm and filling the
   lungs from the bottom NOT the top.

7. Hmmmmming in your nasal resonator
   to clear the nose and sinuses.

8. Last but not least, saying "Thank you!",
   to the Universe for giving you this
   opportunity to share your wisdom
   and an even bigger "Thank You!" to the
   audience who eagerly came to hear you
   and stayed until you were done!

CHAPTER 7

Voice And The Telephone.. "Hello!"

Someone gave him the gift of gab! He should go and exchange it for a shirt!

How much of your day is spent on the telephone? Counting the work place and home, we can spend hour after hour with that plastic "thing" glued to our ear.

Case in Point!

I was casually shopping in a department store the other day when out of nowhere, a telephone rang... The lady standing beside me going through the size "8's" reached into her purse, and pulled out a cell phone.

While standing next to me and without missing a beat shuffling the rack, she proceeded to argue with her husband as to who was responsible for taking the kids to a baseball game and whose schedule was the fullest. Her voice was loud and shrill to begin with, but as her emotional temperature began to rise, you could hear her throughout the entire store. No matter where I went, my peaceful airspace was shattered by her penetrating telephone voice. The funny thing was, although everyone in the store could hear her, she was completely oblivious to the fact that she was...

OBNOXIOUS!!!!!

On the telephone, we fight, profess our love, close gigantic business deals, lose large sums of money, receive good news, and too often receive bad news. Some of the most important events of our lives occur over the telephone.

Telephone conversations can be very emotional and extremely stressful. It's no wonder this often leads to vocal problems at the end of a long day.

Once upon a time we could get into our car and close out the world with all of its ringing telephones, but no more. The ever present cell phone has made it possible for people to find us 24 hours a day no matter where we are.

As you have learned in the chapter on emotions, each of life's events, good or bad, causes a reaction in the vocal cords. Be it a tightening of the cords or a lifting of the larynx, (the lump thing again), this constant adjusting eventually takes its toll on the voice.

Emotions that tighten the vocal cords:

- **Anger**
- **Excitement**
- **Sorrow**
- **Frustration**
- **Resentment**

Emotions that soften the vocal cords:

- **Love**
- **Tenderness**

Emotions that lighten the vocal cords:

- **Happiness**
- **Joy**

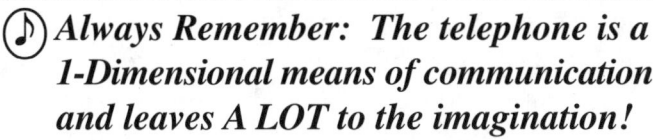

Always Remember: The telephone is a 1-Dimensional means of communication and leaves A LOT to the imagination!

Being an *audio* device with *no visual* whatsoever, it is vital we project the correct vocal image over those fiber-optic cables that go directly to the ear and imagination of the person on the other end.

In the business world, very seldom do we actually meet, let alone see, the people we do business with every day. Your concept of the man in the shipping department with the wonderful deep voice is that he looks like Tom Selleck (works for me!) or the lady in accounting who's gentle voice always reminds you of your great aunt Edna (on your father's side).

How important is the telephone voice? It can actually make or break a career. That's how important it is. People have been known to fall in love with just a "voice" on the other end of the telephone.

Voices that can affect us and push our buttons:

- **Warm and friendly**
- **Sympathetic**
- **Stern**
- **Business like**
- **Cold and detached**
- **Motherly or fatherly (nurturing)**
- **Angry**
- **Frustrated**
- **Sexy**

Voices not only affect us emotionally, but they can influence our physical actions as well. The right sounding voice can persuade us to buy a house, switch our phone service, use a product, call a lawyer to sue them when the product stinks, slam the phone down on them, and even give them our money if they are good talkers. This is especialy true and we are *especialy* vulnerable if they have a voice we trust like great aunt Edna (on your father's side).

> ♪ *There is a lot of uncertainty and fear of the unknown connected to the telephone.*

When someone cannot see us and they do not know who we are, we can step outside of ourselves and become whomever we choose to be. The person on the other end of the telephone will never know the difference. I am one of those people who have a dread of using the telephone. I have a tendency to avoid calling people back, and I have even been known to hang up when they answer, especially when I didn't expect them to be home.

The last time I did that, the person on the other end had caller ID. They called me right back and said, "Why did you hang up on me?" Feeling like a kid with her hand in the cookie jar, I mumbled something about my telephone not working right and I never did that again. Caller ID cured me of a rude habit, but I still have the fear.

Your Telephone Personality

What is all of this leading up to? We simply need to be more aware of how others perceive us over the telephone. It is important to know your own telephone personality. I have a male friend whose voice is very breathy. Every time he leaves a message it sounds like an obscene phone call. Like the lady who annoyed an entire store with her voice, he doesn't even know the negative effect of his voice on the phone.

Let's take a look at some of the major problems we encounter in our everyday interaction with the telephone:

A good place to start is a *reality check of your own telephone voice.* I want to emphasize the word *telephone* because many of us completely change voices when our hand reaches for the receiver.

I know a woman whose natural voice personality is brusque and business like. She becomes a *butter-would-melt-in-your-mouth* personality when the telephone rings. I also know a man whose natural voice personality is very stern. He becomes gentle and fatherly when he is speaking on the telephone, especially if the person on the other end is a female.

Loving your own voice

How we hear ourselves is not how others hear us. By the time the voice has traveled out the mouth and back to the ears, it can become very distorted.

Even tape recording the voice misses many of the natural overtones found in a "live" voice. Especially a small tape recorder like the ones that live in our answering machines. Remember the bigger the speaker, the bigger the sound! That tiny speaker cannot possibly give you an accurate reading of your natural sounding voice.

I am not suggesting you go out and buy an expensive tape recorder to do this exercise, I merely want you to be aware that what you hear is only a *part of how you sound.* It's a bit like seeing what you actually look like. To your eyes, all you have ever seen of yourself is a one-dimensional picture or a flat mirror image.

You will never be able to see yourself as others see you! It is exactly the same with the voice, you can not hear the overtones in your voice others hear. So with that in mind, when doing the following exercise, be **analytical** of your voice, **not critical!**

Recording the Voice Exercises:

Settle down in a nice, quiet place where you will not be disturbed for at least 30 minutes, and please, leave your cell phone in the car. Read the following verse out loud into you tape recorder. Listen with an honest ear as if it were some one else's voice. Write down what you hear and practice changing what you don't like about the voice you hear. Is it too low, too high, too fast, boring, etc. This will help you to "know" your voice better and what areas need improvement.

Hiawatha

First he danced a solemn measure,

Very slow in step and gesture,

In and out among the pine trees,

Treading softly like a panther.

Then more swiftly and still swifter,

Whirling, spinning round in circles,

Till the leaves went whirling with him,

Till the dust and leaves together

Spread in eddies round about him.

Henry Wodsworth Longfellow

Now, play it back and rate your vocal performance. Was your speaking voice:

- **Too soft**
- **Monotone**
- **Too fast**
- **Too harsh**
- **Too high-pitched**
- **Emotionless**
- **Too boring**
- **Too slow and drawn out**
- **Too muffled (No articulation)**
- **Nasal**

Let's give it a try on the answering machine:

Record a new message on your machine and play it back. Again, be the analyst, not the critic... Put yourself in the "ears" of the person on the other end of the telephone and be honest about what you are hearing. Does the voice you hear sound:

- **Warm and friendly**
- **Detached and cold**
- **Intelligent and trusting**
- **Mature**
- **Sympathetic**
- **Impatient**
- **Angry**
- **Sexy**

Developing an Awesome Telephone Voice

Now that you have a pretty good idea of what you actually sound like on the other end of a telephone, here are a few tips to improve your telephone voice:

Tip #1
Take a moment before making an important call to analyze it and find your "motivation" (as they say in acting school). What reaction do you want from the person on the other end? How do you want them to perceive you?

Using the list of voice characteristics on the previous page, and realizing that what you choose to send through the wire is what they will get, practice the voice you want them to hear. Stay focused no matter what comes back at you. (All the world is a stage etc., etc., etc.)

Tip #2
If you find your voice cold and unfriendly, the easiest way to lighten it up is to actually put a smile on your face. (Come on, it won't crack.) This smile not only makes you feel better, but the person on the other end will respond in a much friendlier way.

As you put that smile on your face, visualize the person on the other end also smiling. It is impossible to frown and smile at the same time! If you would like to hear the difference a smile makes, record a message on your answering machine with your

regular voice, then record a message using your smiling voice. You will definitely notice the difference.

Tip #3

"Excuse me, but I didn't hear what you said." If that response happens to you frequently, chances are your voice falls into the "too soft" category.

The telephone receiver is actually an amplifier, but because it will not carry high frequencies beyond 3000Hz, many of the low tones are filtered away, especially in an inexpensive telephone. This makes the voice difficult to understand if the voice is soft and low.

The solution to this problem is almost as simple as putting a smile on your face. Because the telephone receiver is a microphone, the best solution to a soft voice is to speak into it as if you were giving your commencement speech in college. Talk directly into the receiver. If people continue having difficulty understanding you, it may be time to invest in a better telephone.

Tip #4

Tension in the voice is very easy to identify and usually comes to those who have a fear of the telephone. If that is you, when the telephone rings take a moment before you answer it to "pant breathe" (you learned to do it in chapter three). This will relax the cords. A good old "yawn sigh" will do wonders also.

In the middle of a heated, emotional conversation, if you feel that throat "lump" coming and your pitch starts to rise, say, "Excuse me one moment," cover the receiver and yawn sigh (Ahhhhhhhhhhh) everything back down again. As an added bonus, this will give your emotions a much needed break. Cool down time is wonderful!

Tip #5
Are you one of those oblivious blasters? (If you're not sure, ask your friends and family to tell you. If they know you really mean it, they'll gladly tell you.)

One of the main reasons for an overly loud voice is the speaker may be hard of hearing. When all your friends have lovingly told you over and over again that you speak too loudly, it would be a good time to visit an audiologist for a hearing test. If your hearing is fine, then you must learn to be more sensitive to the noise levels around you, unless you are simply talking loud to get attention. If that's the case... GROW UP!!!

Here is a good way to break the "loud habit." When the telephone rings, pretend there is a baby sleeping in the next room. If you wake him up, you'll have to change him and put him back to sleep. (There goes your peace and quiet...) You'd better speak softly. Remember the telephone receiver is an amplifier. YOU DON'T NEED TO SHOUT.

Tip #6

Last but not least, let's address the "talking too fast" problem. A sure sign this means you is when people constantly ask you to repeat what you say. "Excuse me, but I didn't catch what you said." Or "Would you mind repeating that please? I didn't quite get it." Or, "Huh?"

In working with people who talk too fast, I have found the most effective tool is a trick used by actors whose every word must be understood. The trick is to put a silent "beat" between the words that need slowing down. To slow down an entire paragraph, also add the beats at the end of each sentence. Here is an exercise to help you slow down:

"And the Beat Goes On" Exercise...

"Good evening ladies and gentlemen. (beat) Tonight I am going to speak to you about (beat) apprehension. (beat beat) When John Glen, (beat) who as you all know was the first astronaut in space, (beat) was asked what his thoughts were as he was lifting off of the earth, (beat beat) he replied with a laugh, (beat beat beat) "I looked around me (beat) and all I could think of was, (beat beat beat) everything in this ship was built by the lowest bidder." (Now wait for the audience to respond. Ha ha ha ha ha.) "Now that's what I call (beat) apprehension. (beat beat) Speaking of apprehension, (beat) did you ever hear the one about...

...And On!"

Take your prepared script and insert the"beats" before you begin to learn it. Always use a pencil because you may change your mind regarding where each beat is most effective in your talk. Speak your script and where there is a beat, clap your hands. This will help you to feel the beats as pauses. Always give people time to answer you mentally if you ask a question:

"How are you folks doing tonight?" In your mind, listen for their response, ("We are doing fine.") That takes up about 2 beats of time, then go on with your talk..." Tonight I am going to talk about apprehension, etc. etc...

Before we leave this chapter on the telephone voice, it is important to mention telephone posture for those of you who do most of your work over the phone. Look at these two examples:

Telephone Posture

Example Number One	Example Number Two
Wrong	**Right**

In example number one: The entire weight of the head is smashing down on the larynx. This puts tremendous weight on the vocal cords, which in turn forces them to work twice as hard to get the job done. By the end of the day, the pressure has built up and the cords will shut down to protect themselves. If you continue to force them to perform under this handicap you will be left with a raspy, breathy voice at the end of your working day.

This situation often occurs when you are reading text over the telephone. The solution is to buy yourself an inexpensive book stand to put your papers on so the head can stay in a relaxed, upright position. (As shown in example number two.)

In number two the chin is lifted up and the cords are free to adjust without the added weight. **Caution: Do not lift the chin too far up and activate the "swallow guys" or you could start that whole swallowing chain reaction discussed in chapter three.** Once again, just follow your mother's advice and: "*Sit up straight!*

CHAPTER 8

Age And The Voice

You know you're getting older when your idea of an early dinner is lunch.

As the Baby Boomers come of age, they bring with them a major focus on staying youthful. I am right in there with them, so I was really looking forward to researching the latest information on keeping the voice young for this chapter.

Hoping this particular chapter would be a major contribution to my literary masterpiece, I began by reading everything I could get my hot little hands on regarding aging and the voice. Of course, I have my own opinion based on my years of teaching both male and female voices of all ages, but it's always good to have verification from the medical experts. (A little "I knew that!" is *so* good for the ego.)

After plowing through numerous books on aging and books on voice, it didn't take me long to realize that most experts do not consider the voice when addressing the aging process. If they do, they simply follow the standard researched data on the subject.

Even the top voice research experts like Dr. Daniel R. Boone complain about how little research is being done on this very important part of our human anatomy. (By the way, I recommend Dr. Boone's book, *Is Your Voice Telling on You?,* for anyone with voice problems.)

My own experience with a voice "expert" left me feeling hopeless with nowhere to turn.

As I stated in the beginning of this book, I came into the teaching world of voice as one who needed desperately to "fix" my own voice problems. These problems were creating panic in my career, so I made an appointment with one of the leading voice specialists at that time. Money was no object, I desperately needed my voice fixed.

After spending a few minutes looking down my throat, the Doctor slowly put the instrument in his hand on the small table in front of him, looked me straight in the eye and said, "Well, Joni, what can you expect at your age? This could be a good time for a career change." With that, he got up and left the room.

I sat there with my career passing before my eyes asking the musical question, " Could my voice just wear out?"

That was 20 years ago!

So many people are still of the belief that an aging voice is a "fact of life." Have you ever done an imitation of an older person speaking? You probably made your voice high pitched and wobbly while your friends doubled over with laughter. Well, shame on you, because that is simply an outdated stereotype and it is completely wrong!

Oh, I'm sure if you visit your grandmother at her retirement home, you will find some of the residents who actually sound like that, **BUT HEAR THIS WELL:**

🎵 ***High pitched, wobbly voices come from years of abusing the voice, NOT AGE!***

Yes, the vocal cords are delicate mucous membranes, but if you treat them with the love and respect they deserve, they will last you a lifetime.

So many factors affect the performance of your vocal cords. If you continually smoke, take drugs (prescription or not), inhale toxic chemicals, yell excessively at sports events, and overuse the voice day after day, year after year, some of the parts are just going to wear down and out.

With excessive abuse, the vocal cords will wear out long before you reach old age, like mine did. I was incorrectly trying to out-sing a very loud big band without a prayer of coming out on top. (More on vocal abuse in the next chapter.)

Through the years: A flashback

From the Mars/Venus chapter, you will remember how boys and girls start life with the same size cords and the same high voice pitch. Then, during puberty, when the hormones rage, boys with an overload of testosterone experience an elongation of the cords causing an eight note (octave) drop in pitch. Girls also experience a smaller pitch drop of four notes. (For a review of how this works, go back to page 120 and "sing the voice drops" with Julie Andrews and Doe Re Me.)

After the voice drops during puberty, the hormone levels stabilize and the voice stays the same for the middle years of life (except during those "Grace Days" for women mentioned in chapter five).

Following mid-life, the hormones again begin to change, and the voice starts another transition. For women, it begins with menopause. The estrogen levels drop and the testosterone levels rise. This causes the cords to thicken and the voice to deepen.

As traumatic as this is for a woman who begins to sound like a man, it is equally traumatic for a man who begins to sound like a woman.

As his glorious, manly testosterone level begins to wane after the age of 70, the man's cords begin to thin and his voice begins to rise.

I find this an ironic state of affairs. Vocally, both sexes start out the same, separate in puberty, stabilize in mid-life and switch positions in the last inning.

> # *Don't tell me God doesn't have a sense of humor!!*

Now for some more good news!

> (♪) *With proper voice technique and good healthy care of your body, your voice should only get better as you age. YES!!!*

To prove the point, I have students 16 years of age whose voices shake and wobble more than my 70 year old students.

As for my own experience, I decided not to take the advice of the throat specialist to find another career. Today my voice is stronger than it ever was. I still sing with a 15 piece big band, only now I don't try to out shout them. My voice is as strong after four hours of singing as it was at the beginning of the night. Knowledge is a powerful tool!! Here are 10 great things you can do to keep your own voice young and healthy.

Joni's "Top 10" List of Things to Do to Keep the Voice Young.

NUMBER TEN

Never believe anyone who says the voice will change as you grow older. Your voice mechanism has no individual brain. It believes what you believe. To change the quality of your voice life, start by changing what you believe about it.

NUMBER NINE

Include the voice in your daily exercise. Go to the chapter on the diaphragm and do your breathing exercises everyday. The voice is a wind instrument. Keep your breathing parts strong and the voice will stay strong.

NUMBER EIGHT

Drink plenty of water each day to keep the vocal cords hydrated. A constant dry throat causes fraying at the edge of the cords. Try breathing through your nose sometimes instead of always through your mouth. This allows the air to become warm and moist before it ever reaches your cords.

NUMBER SEVEN

If you must take prescription drugs, always ask your doctor what side effects they could have on your vocal cords. Any diuretic or decongestant is going to dry up the mucous that coats the cords. If you know that, you can drink warm tea and suck on lemon drops to keep the voice from going dry when you are speaking. (Sugarless drops will do just fine for the weight conscious.)

NUMBER SIX
Watch your posture! As we get older the weight of the world seems to pull us down. ("They" say it's a gravity thing.) Keep the area between your rib cage and your hip bones lifted, especially if you are one of those people who sits at the job all day.

When the midsection is collapsed, the diaphragm cannot do its work and the breath is not free. This not only causes your belly to "pooch *out*" *but restricts the air flow through the vocal cords. When the breath is tight and shallow, the voice will be tight and shallow.*

NUMBER FIVE
Always be aware of the noise level wherever you are. If you find yourself at a "Rolling Stones revival concert," do not, I repeat, do not try to shout over those huge speakers. There is nothing you have to say that can't wait. If you're afraid you'll forget, carry a notebook and write it down. Nothing you have to say is worth damaging the voice.

NUMBER FOUR
Avoid constant clearing of the throat. Every time you scrape those cords together you cause a bit of damage. It would be like constantly scraping the scab off of a wound. If you continued to do that year after year, imagine what that wound would look like. (Sorry for that picture.) Clearing the throat year after year takes its toll on the voice.

NUMBER THREE
Keep your pitch up in the voice when you are depressed. Constant speaking from the bottom of the throat weighs the

voice down and causes the cords to thicken. A youthful voice has a lift to it. Keep your spirits up. Think youthful, and the voice will follow your thought.

Remember, (one more time) the voice parts have no brain; If you believe in a lifted, light voice the voice parts will follow your lead.

NUMBER TWO
Take at least a half hour each day to completely relax your body and your voice. (Remember: Your voice IS your body!) Try a yoga class. Learn to meditate. Do a self-hypnosis session, or just take the time to sit in a quiet beautiful spot and talk to no one.

The voice holds all of our emotions in its little hands and gives them back to us when we talk. Take that few minutes each day and *don't talk at all*, (especially if you're a talker's talker). This is the greatest gift you can give to your voice. The voice can even be affected by your emotions when you're not talking. So along with don't talk, add don't think. Clear your brain every so often and give the voice a much needed rest.

THE NUMBER ONE THING TO DO TO KEEP YOUR VOICE HEALTHY: (Drum Roll Please!)
Don't smoke! Don't drink alcohol. Alcohol is a dehydrator and will dry up your vocal cords. (A bit of wine is fine but not if you are going to talk or sing.) And last but not least. Just say "No" when it comes to drugs. Even some prescription drugs. They wreak havoc on the vocal cords as well as on your life!! (This subject is covered in chapter nine, "When to Take Your Voice to the Doctor.") This is not to say that you can't "get down and party hearty" every once in a while... Letting off steam is great for the stress factor, but not the night before a big presentation. Be wise and treat your voice and your body with respect!

To wrap it up

When it comes to *age and the voice*, wisdom, understanding and correct action will always win over stereotypes and incorrect medical prognosis.

It has taken many years for the voice to come to the attention of researchers, but they are beginning to believe the voice does not have to deteriorate and switch genders with age.

For many years, when it came to the physical body, people believed, **"What *is, is!"*** Now they are beginning to see, **"What *is, may NOT be what has to be*!"** (Does that make sense to you? It sure does to me!)

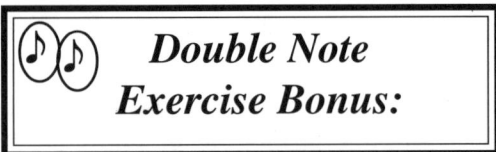

Double Note Exercise Bonus:

Here is an exercise to increase your wind power, lift your spirits and strengthen the abdominal diaphragm:

The "Whistle Technique"

There are three requirements to this exercise:

✔ You have to know how to whistle.

✔ You need a radio, tape or CD player in your car.

✔ You need to practice this at home first.

Pucker up, Let's go...

Begin by checking your posture. Be sure you are sitting up straight in your car seat. (The back support should be all the way up in "Little old lady from Pasadena" position.) The abdominal diaphragm is lifted up out of the rib cage. Check the space between your last rib and your hip bones. The longer the space, the more lifted you will be and the freer the diaphragm is to pump the air you will need to whistle with...

Place your hands on the steering wheel... (This is a much safer activity while driving than talking on your cell phone because both of your hands are on the steering wheel). Now begin:

1. First pant like a dog to get your pump working. Always begin the breathing process by filling the pump before letting the air out. (See chapter three The abdominal diaphragm .)

2. After your panting action is in full working order... in with the air... out with the air... in... out... in... out etc., you are ready for the fun part, but first...

Important!!

♪ *The panting must be even or there will be a tendency to hyperventilate causing dizziness. If you feel the slightest bit of light headedness while panting, stop immediately until the feeling passes. DO NOT DRIVE IF YOU BECOME THE LEAST BIT DIZZY. As you become an expert panter and learn to regulate your breath, this dizziness will go away. Remember to take tiny "sips" of air. No more than a thimble full. This exercise does not need a lot of air, it needs regulated air.*

3. Turn on the radio to your favorite easy listening station or pop in your best tape or CD. When a song comes on that you know the melody to, begin the following whistle technique. (Slow ballads with simple melodies are best. The National Anthem also works great, but don't stand up!.)

Male and female pitch ranges are very different so guys should stick to guy songs and girls should stick to girl songs for this exercise.

As you get good at this exercise, make yourself a practice tape of your favorite "whistle" songs. (Hard rock is not recommended for this exercise, but if "Twisted Sister" is your passion, give it a try.)

4. *With your lips in a whistle position, your back straight, both hands on the wheel and your abdominal diaphragm lifted and free, place the tip of your tongue against the bottom teeth and begin to pump the air in and out... Now, add the melody of the song to the air you are pumping.*

This is not like a regular whistle because the sound is on both the "in" air and the "out" air. In a regular whistle, the sound is only on the outgoing air. Also, to know the melody perfectly is not important. Be as creative with your melody as you choose to be. This exercise is about strengthening the abdominal diaphragm and learning to regulate the air that it pumps, not musical ability. Do not analyze!

5. *Ignore the staring people in the car next to you at the stop light. Just wave a hand but do not smile or you will lose your "whistle."*

Do not get discouraged. Some songs "whistle" better than others. Practice makes ... well not perfect, but it makes it more fun.

6. *Keep that air pumping With each pump of the abdominal diaphragm, the muscles will build strength. Remember to watch for any "light headedness."*

If you feel dizzy stop pumping the air and go back to talking on your cell phone!

♪Voice Notes♪

CHAPTER 9

When To Take Your Voice To the Doctor

A man sat in a doctor's office and kept up a strange litany: "I hope I'm sick. I hope I'm sick." Another waiting patient asked, "Why do you want to be sick?" The man replied, "I'd hate to be well and feel this bad!"

What good is a piano player without a well-tuned piano, a race car driver without a mechanically maintained car, or a speaker without a functionally balanced voice? We tune our piano to keep it playing beautiful music. We service our car to keep it running smoothly, but when it comes to the voice, very few of us even know when it's in trouble.

The best defense against permanent voice loss is a good understanding of how the voice works and good vocal maintenance. The previous chapters have given you a good understanding of how the voice operates, this chapter is all about maintaining the voice. In other words, how to keep it in good working order.

This is not meant to be a scare chapter decrying all the things that can go wrong with the voice, but in the world of reality, it's best to know who the enemy is. Knowledge is freedom, so let's face the "voice lions" that are causing us the problems.

Colds and Flu

The common cold is called "common" because it affects all of us. Although the symptoms can be very annoying, they are not life threatening and most people do not seek medical help. The exception to this is the man or woman whose livelihood depends on a healthy voice.

With the first sneeze, we reach for the kleenex, a decongestant and a box of menthol cough drops. The only one of these that doesn't affect the vocal mechanism negatively is the kleenex.

The cold is not a bacterial infection, it is a viral infection, spread mostly through hand contact and the air we breathe. We can blame the open window and wear a scarf around our throat when we go out into the chilling air all we want, but the truth is:

> (♪) *You have a cold because someone gave it to You! Thanks a lot!*

Our best defense is not to gasp in fear at the open window, but to get enough sleep, watch our diet and make sure we take time to "chill out" from everyday stress.

If we do wake up in the morning with a cold, a day of bed rest while the body heals itself is the best remedy. Steaming the mucous membranes of the nose and throat with a few drops of eucalyptus oil (any health food store has it) also works wonders. If you do not have a steamer, simply boil water in a pan, drop in a few drops of the oil, place a towel over your head and breath in the healing steam all the way down to the bottom of the lungs.

A word of warning: Do not steam if you are planning on going out in the cold air. When you have a cold, the mucus membranes temporarily lose their ability to make quick adjustments to temperature. Going out while your membranes are vulnerable could lower your resistance even more.

> (♪) *Another definite NO NO if you're going outside is: TAKE NO ASPIRIN!*

Aspirin will make you perspire, which in turn cools off the skin. Outside, the germs are anxiously *"lying in wait for you,"* especially when your natural defenses are down. This is a very important fact for your vocal health because aspirin is such a common remedy for the cold.

Aspirin (acetylsalicylic acid) belongs to the family of antipyretics. Their job is to inhibit the heat regulators of the brain and to a certain degree, they lower body temperature by causing us to perspire.

> (♪) *One of the body's main defenses against infection is to increase the body's temperature, not to lower it.*
>
> (♪) *To bring the body's temperature down by taking aspirin goes against the natural healing process of our body.*

So *why* do we do it? Because someone told us it was good for us! Aspirin and related drugs are only good for easing pain but have no effect on the virus and often do us much more harm then good.

What to do with all that liquid that's *"on the run"* when we have a cold is a big problem when you are a speaker or singer. Taking decongestants to dry up the mucus again works against nature's healing forces. Congestion of the mucous membranes and the nasal discharge that goes with it, believe it or not, is part of the healing process. Mucous brings the healing forces of the blood to the infected area and helps the body fight the germs. If you over medicate with drugs that dry up the mucous, you will only make the cold worse.

Another side effect that goes with taking a decongestant to dry up mucous is one that really annoys the voice. A drying agent shows no preference and dries up everything in its path, including the mucous that coats the vocal cords. That's why you get such a scratchy throat with a cold. When we talk excessively on "dried up" vocal cords, we are going to pay the price with the loss of our voice. It isn't necessarily the cold that "scratches" the throat, it's the drying up of its natural lubricating mucous by most cold medications.

What to do? What to do?

Your Mom will tell you to gargle with salt water. Well, don't tell your mom, but gargling is of no use whatsoever. If the gargle is hot, it could help attract blood to the irritated throat and create some healing mucus. Other than that, gargling is only a superficial cleaner.

What about throat lozenges?

No good news here! The glycerine that forms the base of many lozenges dries out the vocal membranes because of its water binding action. Those with menthol in them "chill" the vocal cords with every breath you take through the mouth, and the last thing your cords need is a good "chill." It is warmth, blood flow and mucous that keep them lubricated and in good working condition. The only positive thing I have found about throat lozenges is, they do stimulate the saliva glands. I keep a jar of lemon drops in my studio for the same purpose. A lemon drop can stimulate the saliva glands just by thinking about it and saliva is always the best lubricant for your dry voice parts!

Voltaire, an 18th century
French philosopher wrote:

> (♪) *"Medicine is the art of entertaining the patient while nature takes care of the healing."*

Even with today's medicines, when it comes to the voice and colds, the cure may cause more problems than the cold itself.

To sum it all up, the best defense against the common cold is to keep the body healthy. Under normal circumstances you do not need to see a doctor. Just rest and let the cold play itself out.

I am not qualified to address serious complications that may arise such as severe headaches, high fevers, persistent coughing, bronchitis, etc. These would require the attention of a doctor. If you wish to explore any of these in a more detailed way, there is a wonderful book entitled *Keep Your Voice Healthy* by Friedrich S. Brodnitz, MD. My wish is to give you an overview of what can go wrong so that when you do visit your doctor, you can give him a clearer description of your symptoms. Let's start with...

Laryngitis

There is a big difference between hoarseness and laryngitis! When we end up with no voice, most of us just call it laryngitis. The medical profession calls it *dysphonia*, I call it disaster.

As one of the many who make a living on the merits of my voice, anything that takes it away is worthy of my attention no matter what they call it. But let's call it what it is for clarification.

- **Hoarseness: Is a symptom.**

- **Laryngitis: Is an infection of the larynx.**

- **Dysphonia: Is a medical term for anything causing the loss of the voice that needs a medical term.**

Proper usage of these three terms in one sentence would be:

"The least common of all dysphonias is the hoarseness in acute laryngitis"

We cry "laryngitis" whenever the voice is wounded, no matter what the cause. Even a simple case of vocal abuse from yelling at a sports event is called laryngitis. **Hear this well:**

> *Laryngitis is an infection of the larynx and is NOT caused by abusing the voice. Vocal abuse is a "bowing" of the vocal cords due to excessive force and is NOT caused by laryngitis. Got it???*

Antibiotics are widely used to treat many types of bacterial infections, but if the infection is a virus, antibiotics are useless. Overuse of antibiotics at the first sign of a cold can cause other problems to arise in the respiratory system. One main problem is the development of strains of "germs" that have learned to live with antibiotics. Be cautious if you are prescribed an antibiotic for your voice problems. Be sure it is an infection, not a virus or simply vocal strain.

How can you know the difference if you are not a trained doctor? Use the process of elimination, and you can get a pretty accurate diagnoses most of the time. **For example:**

CASE #1

If you were at a football game cheering on your favorite team yesterday and today you woke up with a sore throat, there is a very good chance it is just a case of vocal abuse, not laryngitis.

CASE #2

If you are under an extreme amount of pressure at work. If your body is tired, and your defenses are down because you do not take the time to rest or eat properly, chances are you're suffering from voice fatigue, not laryngitis.

CASE #3

Everyone in your office is coughing and sneezing in your air space. You tried to avoid them but this morning you woke up with a scratchy throat. More likely than not, you have a virus that is going around, not laryngitis.

CASE #4

You're on a promotional tour for your new book flying the "red eye" from New York to Denver. You get off the plane and your voice sounds dry and crackly. Your first major TV interview is in three hours and you think, "Oh no! Laryngitis!" Wrong again. It was the cabin pressure in the airplane playing havoc with your vocal cords.

Can you see how very important it is to know how the voice works, and its maintenance, before running to the nearest doctor for a shot of antibiotic?

In my own moments of panic and confusion when wondering what to do as the *Big Date* comes upon me and I have no voice to face it with, I have turned to doctors, medical books, holistic healers, hypnotherapists, acupuncturist, psychic healers, past life regressors, good old fashioned prayer, and listening to my own healing heart. (Phew)

I always found prevention to be the best medicine. As I learn more about the human voice, I am able to avoid more of the pitfalls that lead to poor vocal health, simply by making better choices.

Here is my favorite list
of *Do's* and *Don'ts*...

1. At the first sign of a cold or flu, *DO* rest, rest, rest. The body's natural healing system is better than anything man has come up with yet.

2. Liquids are very important to hydrate the dry cords. Your body is creating mucous to help it heal. *DO* give it plenty of water to work with.

3. Remember, *DON'T* take aspirin if you are going out in the cold air.

4. *DON'T* clear your throat with a vengeance. The more you clear the mucous out, the more mucous you'll have. If you must clear the throat, do it gently.

5. *DON'T* **use cough drops or lozenges with menthol in them. Herbal drops work great and are much better for the cords.**

6. If you are diagnosed with acute or chronic laryngitis by your doctor, *DON'T* **talk or use the voice. Especially** *DON'T* **whisper. Whispering can cause a greater strain on the vocal cords than talking.**

7. *DO* **drink herbal teas. There are some wonderful medicinal teas you can purchase from your health food store that are soothing and calming to a dry, sore throat. My personal favorite is Throat Coat. (Traditional Medicinals.)**

Avoid acids (fruit juices) and anything with caffeine in it. Caffeine is a dehydrator and will dry, not moisten the cords.

8. *DON'T* **over use antibiotics. Only take them if you have a bacterial infection, not a viral infection.**

9. *DO* **inhale steam and eucalyptus oil to soothe the vocal membranes. Heat is a natural healer. To combine the two, take a hot relaxing shower, and inhale the warm moist steam as deep down in the lungs as you can get it.** *DON'T* **go out in the cold air afterwards.**

10. *DO* see your doctor for any of these chronic disorders:

- **Upper respiratory infections**
- **Persistent coughing**
- **Lower respiratory tract infection**
- **Extreme fever**
- **Any symptom that will not go away**
- **Allergies and sinus problems that linger**
- **Tonsillitis**

DO GO TO BED

AND ENJOY THE REST!

Ahhh Choo

When spring comes into bloom, so do the allergies. I have found, as a general rule, allergies do not affect the voice. Sometimes the singing voice gets even better when sinuses are filled with all that water. It causes a resonance in the upper nasal cavity. (Personally I love that resonant voice with a buzz in it.)

As to the physical symptoms of allergies, like watery eyes, headache, etc., I know they are uncomfortable, but we are talking voice here. Allergy medicines have a greater negative effect than the allergies themselves. Allergy medications are designed to "dry up" mucous (here we go again) that in turn dries up the vocal cords.

I can hear the dissenters now, but I stand by my years of working with "voice users" with allergy problems. They come in crying "bad voice day," and more often than not, leave singing better than ever. **Don't you just LOVE IT!**

> (♪) *There is a lot of misinformation out there about the voice for the belief system to pick up.*

Someone once said, "You spot it, you got it!" That is so true regarding the health of the voice. The system is so mentally vulnerable to information, and because we don't know what to believe, we grasp at anything out there whether it's true or not.

I always tell the people I work with to listen to their own logic and see what works for them. If what you hear makes sense to you, do it. If it doesn't make sense, don't do it just because someone says to do it. Your voice is too important to blindly follow orders that do not feel right. This also includes what I say to you. If it does not make sense or feel right, DON'T DO IT!

The Air We Breathe

One of the major offenders in our every day voice life is the very air we breathe. This is especially true in polluted cities where the first ingredient in smog is smoke. Smoke from car exhaust, factories, wood and coal burning fireplaces and the worst one of all, second hand cigarette smoke. The second ingredient is fog. Put them both together and they make smog.

Going back to smoke, I can think of nothing that trashes a voice faster than sitting next to someone who blows smoke in your air space. The only thing worse for your voice than second hand smoke is being the smoker. To fill page after page on the merits of *not* smoking would *not* be productive here, especially when the smoker does not wish to quit. I will only say in regards to your voice;

☛ *SMOKING IS THE WORST THING YOU CAN DO TO YOUR VOICE, PERIOD!!*

Besides the obvious effects of smoking, like lung cancer, throat cancer and mouth cancer, it impairs your breathing, shrinks your vocal range, and ages the voice dramatically. Smoking also annoys and endangers those around you, especially the children.

I have worked with children who want to sing with all their hearts but have permanently damaged voices from years of being in the same house and especially the same car, with someone who smokes.

Their voices are "husky and raspy", making it impossible for them to sing higher notes without straining. The vocal cords "leak" air so badly that their speaking voices are also affected. Seeing this effect to smoking first hand and not being able to fix the cause of the vocal problem (the smoker), is very frustrating to me and devastating to the kids. Sometimes it gets so bad that to save a precious little voice, I have to say something to the parent or grandparent, so here goes...

♪♪♪ *PLEASE, OH PLEASE... Those of you who insist on smoking around young children, be aware of the consequences!!*

The toxins those kids are inhaling are doing damage to the voice and *MAY NOT* be reversible. If you want to smoke, especially in the confines of your car, think first of the precious cargo sitting next to you, and chew gum instead. Isn't this another good reason for you to quit? Then you can *use that breath to sing* in the car with your children. That's much better for you both!

Another "Air" Alert!!!

Don't we all love those brisk, clear, sunny winter days that are so good for our body and spirit. I hate to tell you this but they are the worst on your voice. Respiratory infections have a field day during cold, dry spells not during the rainy times when people believe the wetter season brings on more colds.

Those hot muggy days are uncomfortable for the rest of our physical body, but they will do wonders for the voice.

The next time you go out for an invigorating winter walk with your best friend, be aware. Every time you open your mouth during your stimulating conversations, you are inhaling cold dry air which in turn acts like a "blow dryer" on those delicate vocal cords.

(♪) **Learn the fine art of breathing through your nose and apply it to "dry air" situations.**

When you are the listener, not the talker in the conversation, breathing through the nose transforms the cold dry air into warm moist air by the time it gets to your vocal cords. If you are the "mother of all talkers," a few nose-breath pauses may allow someone else to get a word in.

Two very important things that affect the air we breathe are heating systems and air conditioners. All of us would be better off, voice-wise that is, without either of them.

In winter, the blasts of heat from the furnace will dry the cords, especially when you are sleeping. If possible, put an extra blanket on the bed and turn down the heat. Your voice will love you for that one!

As for the air conditioner you can't live without in the summer, it's job is to pull moisture out of the air and replace it with cold, dry air. Oh boy, does it do its job well! The problem is it also, like the furnace, has no respect for anything around it. It just pulls out moisture whereever the moisture lives, and it lives in your vocal cords.

Spending all day talking in a room with the heat or the air conditioning going full blast is disastrous. By the end of the day your voice will have every ounce of moisture drained from it. Your best defense, next to turning them both off, is to drink plenty of water.

Hydrate, Hydrate, Hydrate.

You must drink water, not caffenated sodas, iced tea, or iced coffee. They all dehydrate the cords and the ice will shrink your voice membranes. Just stick to good old water if you have to use the voice. (These actions may seem extreme but remember, this is a book about the human voice and what affects it.) If you are not going to use your voice, have fun and drink whatever your heart desires.

Flying and the Voice

Many of today's jobs involve air travel. Not only is the voice effected by the pressure in the cabin of the airplane, but the voice must also adjust to extreme climate changes.

When traveling from the hot, moist east coast to the crisp, dry climate of Denver Colorado in a few short hours to attend a very stressful meeting, you should be prepared for some physical adjustments in the voice.

Going from climate to climate takes a lot of adjustment in the body, and when stress is an added factor it decreases the body's natural ability to handle the adjustment. This has a definite impact on the voice. The altitude of "Mile High Denver" affects the delicate muscles of the vocal cords as they try to adjust to a lower density of air. Even your intonation, (the rise and fall of your pitch), can be affected. Who would have thought?

One more thing before we leave the traveling voice...

When going from Southern California to Chicago during the winter, we believe (because our mommie's's told us it was true), we should "bundle up" in the cold weather or we will catch a cold. Nothing could be further from the truth. (Sorry Mom.)

Wearing too many heavy layers of clothing will cause the skin to perspire, making it impossible for its natural climate adjusting process to work. This will open you up to all of those "nasty" germs hanging around just waiting for your defenses to come down. Our climate comfort zone is so small (between 76 and 78 degrees, give or take), that we like to carry it with us wherever we go, inside or out. This weakens the body's natural ability to adjust itself. To help it stay strong, allow yourself to feel a little uncomfortable. Begin to expand your comfort zone a few degrees each month, especially when you are sleeping.

✈ For those times when you have no control over the elements, here are a few travel tips:

✈ If you are a speaker, carry with your important stuff a small moisturizer or steamer to transform your night time dry air into warm, moist air.

✈ Always carry water with you on the plane. I know along with "coffee tea or milk," you can get water, but it is always chilled. Ice is not what you want for your vocal cords. Besides, the cups are so small that you may annoy the stewardess by asking her to "fill you up" one time too many. Stay in control! Bring your own water.

✈ When "climate jumping," wear clothing you can shed easily. Keep your layering light and removable. Be aware when your skin starts to "leak," it's just the body's signal to remove a layer. If you perspire easily, you may have to show some restraint. Sitting in the airplane in your undies is not acceptable.

✈ When traveling by air, avoid lengthy conversations with the person sitting next to you if you are facing a day of voice performance, even if its Harrison Ford. Cabin pressure and talking over the drone of the engines will tire and weaken the voice.

Facing those "Naughty" Nodules

"You have nodules on your vocal cords." These are 7 words
that strike terror in the hearts of those of us who make our
living using the voice.

Does this mean surgery and lost work time? Permanent voice
damage? Throat cancer? Is my career over? What are these men-
acing little lumps on my vocal cords and how did they get there
in the first place? These are all the questions that run rampant
through your brain as you frantically search the internet for answers. Let's start from the last question and move back to the
first question.

**Just what are nodules or "nodes" as they are referred to in
clinical circles?** It is generally believed nodules are benign tu-
mors on the vocal cords. Some doctors believe them to be ob-
structed mucous glands, while others call them corns or callouses.
I would have to say, as with many of the aspects involving the
voice, the available information is very controversial and often
confusing.

I am not a medical doctor so I can only speak from my own
research and experience (15 years) in dealing with these "pesky
little varments," no matter what they are called or whose belief
system you follow, all are in agreement with this one fact:

> (♪) *Nodules on the vocal cords are
> caused by one thing and one thing
> only...wrongful use of the voice!
> Singing or speaking, if you got em,
> you are doing it WRONG*

The first signal that something is very wrong here is a lingering hoarseness and a very tired voice at the end of the day.

Blame it on the flu, a cold, sinus infection, laryngitis, etc., etc., bla, bla, bla. If it just won't go away, you can be pretty certain there is "Trouble in River City!"

Constant strain and vocal abuse will cause those precious cords to rub together and create callous like bumps on one or *both* of your vocal cords. They look like this:

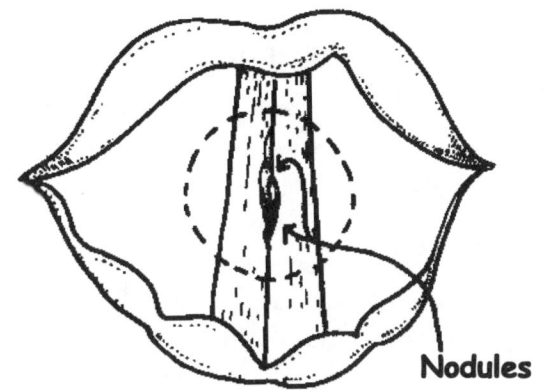

Nodules

Vocal cords

If the doctor's diagnosis is:
"Nodules. Let's operate!"
Run, don't walk to the nearest second opinion.

> (♪) *The cause of the vocal problem is voice abuse and bad vocal technique. The nodule is the effect of the problem, not the cause!!!!!!*

If you remove the effect and *do not* fix the cause, the effect (in this case your nodules,) will only return. This has happened many time to habitual voice abusers.

"OK now what?", you ask.

Before considering surgery, especially if the vocal weakness is relatively new, put yourself in the loving hands of a good speech-language pathologist and overhaul your vocal engine. If you are a singer, find yourself a good vocal coach who has had experience working with singers with nodules and *fixed* them.

> ♪ *If anyone says, "Voice rest will fix it!", this is not the answer. Go find another pair of loving hands to put yourself into.*

Sometimes you have to kiss a lot of frogs to find a prince. Pucker up and keep kissing until you find the right person to work with. Remember, the voice has no brain and can only follow your way of thinking. If you think your therapist isn't right for you, find someone else. The feelings of another person are not important when it comes to the voice. You need positive feedback and no stress so the voice will repair itself and you can get on with your life. The vocal mechanism carries the "weight of your discontent" and too much weight will keep those nodules in your life.

Polyps

Some doctors will diagnose *polyps* on the vocal cords. Like nodules, they are also benign growths. They can reach the size of a cherry stone and carry some of the same symptoms as nodules. Unlike nodules, polyps can move up and down with the breath. They are visible when the voice is forced and then disappear from view when it is relaxed. The voice can go from clear to hoarse as they move about. One examination can spot them, while another will miss them completely, according to where they sit on the cords.

There still is a lot of speculation about the origin of polyps. Most experts believe, like nodules, they are also caused by constant irritation of the cords. This irritation can be from prolonged laryngitis, smoking, and voice abuse.

The usual treatment for polyps is surgical removal. As with nodules, if the original cause is not found (the source of the abuse), they too will return in a few years.

ALERT! ALERT! ALERT!

- **Always get a second or third opinion.**

- **Do your homework and research well before agreeing to any surgery on the vocal cords.**

Recently there have been some "horror stories" of people who have gone *in* to have a simple operation on their vocal cords only and come *out* with no voice at all. Julie Andrews is one who has lost the use of her once beautiful soprano voice to nodule surgery. Her voice problem was caused by the vocal strain of "Belting out" a singing role on Broadway. (Victor Victoria.) The term "to belt" means to sing very loud.

Julie Andrews has a light, high soprano voice and to sing low and loud put too much pressure on the vocal cords creating nodules. Again, surgery is not the answer to an over stressed pair of vocal cords.

If it can happen to "Mary Poppins", it can happen to you! Be aware.

"When Do I See A Doctor?"

> (♪) *If your hoarseness lingers for more than three weeks, it should be looked at by a competent throat specialist.*

In this book I have touched on the effects of misusing the voice. This is the major cause of voice loss, however, there are symptoms and causes that go beyond what we have discussed so far. I will touch briefly on a few of the major ones. If you feel your problem goes beyond what has been covered here, do not hesitate to seek professional help. The voice is precious and must be treated as a delicate part of your body.

Cancer of the Throat

There is a growing fear of cancer in the voice and throat area. Regarding this fear of laryngeal cancer, it is important to know that this type of cancer grows slowly and remains localized for quite awhile. If the growth is small there is a good chance of a cure by operation or radiation. If laryngeal cancer is caught in the early stages, there is also a good chance the voice can be preserved. Everyday there are new breakthroughs in the field of medicine and the voice is beginning to take its place on the list of priorities in medical research.

There is no reason for a cancer scare every time there is a loss of voice. Prolonged vocal abuse does not cause cancer, but it does cause other serious complications .

Smoking causes most cancers in the neck and throat area. I'm a bit sensitive about this because I lost my favorite drummer to cancer of the throat (windpipe). His first symptom was when his incredible singing voice began to lose power and pitch. By the time he sought professional help, it was too late. (But he kept right on puffing on his cigarettes up until the end).

> (♪♫) **When you have the wisdom to know what harms the voice and keep on doing the very thing that causes the problems, the consequences are inevitable.**

Spasmodic Dysphonia
Vocal Cord Paralysis

Before closing this chapter on voice health, I'd like to touch on a rising concern that is receiving a lot of media focus: *Spasmodic dysphonia,* a paralysis of the vocal cords.

On a "Nightline" special report recently, Ted Koppel devoted an entire program to a female radio talk show host who lost the use of her voice and a very successful career. As her voice became weaker and weaker, she went from doctor to doctor looking for an answer to her voice problem. No one could tell her the cause or the cure. To make a long painful story into a short painfully story, she finally was diagnosed with *spasmodic dysphonia.* The solution was injecting a toxic substance called *Botulium toxin or Botox* into her vocal cords. It is the same deadly poison plastic surgeons use to freeze the muscles of the face so they don't wrinkle. She has had 5 injections so far into her vocal cords. No one can tell her what the long term effects may be. According to her own research, there are **thousands** of people suffering from *spasmodic dysphonia.* Oh dear!!!**

The general recommendation for all voice problems is voice therapy before any surgery or injection. In most cases, the vocal muscles will become strong again and surgery or injection will not be needed. Teflon injections are also used in emergency situations when the voice is completely gone. Also steroids are injected into the cords to "plump" them up so they can come together and make sound. All of this "injection stuff" makes me very, very nervous!!

These are not cures to basic voice problems, but they will help the singer to "sing" at the "Academy Awards", and the speaker to do the all-important presentation when the voice is gone. As stated before, no one knows what the long term effects of all of this will be. Be careful with your voice!

> ♪ *No "quick fix" is a substitute for good voice technique!!*

Start now! Do not wait for a "voice problem" to devastate your life before you take action. Keep that in mind if you hear the words *"spasmodic dysphonia"* and *"botulinum toxin"* coming from the mouth of a doctor who is staring down your throat.

(** Her name is Diane Rehm and if you would like more information on the subject of *Spasmodic Dysphonia,* you can contact Ted Koppel, *Nightline* at NBC or read her recently published book, *Finding My Voice by Diane Rehm. Knopf 1999.* You may also visit the website of Dr. Morton Cooper for an in-depth report on voice disorders. Good stuff!)

CHAPTER 10

Tuning Up the Mind, Body and Soul

" I jog everywhere for my health, but I never find it!"
Bumper Sticker

If there is a common theme running through this book, it's this: In order for the voice to function properly and last a lifetime, it takes the complete cooperation of a mighty trio,the voice, the mind and the body. But to bring that voice to life, (ask any singer and they will tell you,) it takes ..

"Soul"

Up until now, this book has been mainly about *the voice*, the *3-Dimensional Voice* to be exact. Now, in order to complete the equation, the other three parts, *mind, body,* and *soul,* must be put in place and tuned to perfection.

Let's start with the thinking part of this unit, the mind/brain.

The brain's job is to give instruction to the individual parts of the voice unit. Those precious parts already know how to do their job, but they need something to tell them *when, where, and why.* In other words, as magnificent as this voice instrument is, *it still needs that skilled player to play it.* I constantly tell my students, "The vocal cords have no brain, they will believe what you believe!" If you believe there is a limit to your vocal power, and live that belief, the voice is forced to perform in the limitations of that belief. People who come into the studio saying "I love to sing, but I have no voice," have lived an entire life denying themselves the gift of song. It is such fun when they find out they are:

WRONG!

The mind has a broader scope of vision than the brain and functions in the intuitive field. It feeds the brain choices beyond what the brain can deduce from its own thinking resources. (The musically "gifted" can reach beyond the brain and pull from the creative, intuitive side of the mind.) Sometimes the brain is so stuck in a belief, it does not want to open up to new input and choices. It keeps insisting the old ways are better and programs all of the voice parts accordingly.

I have found in my teaching that if I can keep the brain busy and out of its old patterns, it will allow the new information to "sneak" in. Then when the results bring improvement to the voice, and the brain knows *that it works,* it will change its opinion and the new information becomes part of the thinking process.

As illustrated earlier, when you re-program your thinking about the voice, the voice mechanism takes over and does its job without any interference. The old saying *"Keep an open mind,"* should be, *"Keep an open brain."*

> ♪ *The beauty of the human thought process is that it is ever expanding. It is always looking for new ways to solve old problems.*

Unless of course, you have a very stubborn brain, then you continue with the old ways that don't work and keep facing the same problems over and over again. The voice is a relatively new frontier for the brain, it needs a bit of loving patience from you.

For those of you who just said, "Oh come on. Isn't that just New Age mumbo jumbo?" I have to say to you, I have watched this process happen so many times and it has become common practice in my world for people to sing notes they previously believed were out of their vocal ranges. It's like running the four minute mile, once someone did it, others will follow.

I have worked with many a stubborn brain and had to give it the same information five different ways before it said, "I'll be darned, this works. Why didn't you just say that in the first place." (Yeah, sure!)

The Mozart Effect

Researchers are finding new ways to crack the stubborn brain every day. Recently I attended a San Diego Symphony concert featuring music from *The Mozart Effect*, a book written by Don Campbell on research he has been doing since 1988 combining the music of Mozart and the human brain process.

This research shows amazing results using Mozart's music to stimulate the learning abilities of people of all ages, with and without learning disabilities.

His is one of many projects involving opening the left brain (the learning side), and using an outside influence to stimulate its learning capabilities. Music is one of the most influential ways of doing that.

Go turn on some Mozart and shelve the rock and roll while you are studying. Your brain will love you for it! And so will your neighbors. **Let's go deeper within ...**

The Soul

> ♪ *The Greek philosopher Galen said:*
> *"The voice is the mirror of your soul."*

How true! All that you believe is implanted in your voice. That is why lie detector tests are given. By measuring the pitch and movement of your voice, they can tell if you are lying or telling the truth.

The external words you say are meaningless "jabber." Politicians and lawyers lie every day and get away with it. They don't care as long as we believe their words. The interesting thing about testing a voice is that the words can lie, but even the best of them cannot hide the truth from the voice.

When the voice feels the lying words, (remember the voice can feel your true emotions no matter what your words are saying), the voice temperature rises, and the larynx goes up taking the pitch and everything else up with it. This causes erratic movement in the voice that can be measured by the experts. Isn't that incredible? The voice cannot tell a lie.

Our emotions are the part of us deeply implanted in our belief systems. We program our emotions to react to events based on all of our previous experiences. The voice reacts to those emotional responses.

When it is asked to speak the truth, the voice speaks from the internal emotion not from the external words. It should be mandatory in an election year that during those great political debates each candidate be hooked to a lie detector so we could know his *internal truth*. Then we could all make better choices.

Voice and the Personality

Did you know certain voices have certain personality traits? People who make their living reading people (I don't mean psychic readers, I mean well trained business people), study how we talk and treat us accordingly. Our voices are used to study trends in advertising, buying habits, demographics etc. We are continuously being judged and categorized in some way by the sound of our voice.

The following examples of personality voice traits are used by many sales and business professionals. If you have ever gone to a sales promotional seminar, body language is a big factor in "closing a sale." Right up there with body language sits our voice personality analysis.

On the following page, see if you can find yourself among the examples. Don't take it personal, but do take it to heart, because this is how you are be judged by those people who "map" our destinies.

Let's See Where You Fit In. Are You...

A **Slow Talker**: This trait is categorized as someone who is sure of themselves. Slow talkers think carefully before offering an opinion. A slow speaker often has an exaggerated opinion of his or her own importance. They demand everyone pay attention to what they say and drag the conversation out as long as they can stay in control. They are born leaders and often egotistical.

A Fast Talker: This can signal an overactive brain or a shallow personality. Speaking a steady stream of superficial small talk and never giving another a chance to participate is a call for attention and control. It is the sign of a person who takes little thought for another's opinion.

A Deep Voice: Can be either a naturally low pitched instrument or someone needing to express authority. Often a young lawyer or minister will lower the voice to appear older and wiser. (This can cause major voice problems if done incorrectly. See *"The First Dimension, Depth"* in chapter three). A deep voice is associated with authority. When someone is *naturally* blessed with a wonderful, resonant, deep voice, the opportunities are endless.

A Loud Voice: This expresses energy and confidence without self criticism. People who are loud are often self-centered and demand a lot of attention.

A Soft Voice: Will instantly signal a lack of self confidence and the feeling that no one wants to hear what you have to say anyway. These are people who do not speak up when they should and can often be led into business dealings they should never be in. They can't say,

NO!

If you were looking for that "fast sale" to win the trip to Mexico, as a business person, wouldn't you head straight for the soft talker who just "can't" say no?

> ## How would you like to do your own research project?

Begin your research by becoming more aware of voices around you. See if you can detect emotional changes in pitch. Listen to the voices and see if what the experts say about the personality traits match the personalities connected to the voices. Where do you fit in?

One of the great frustrations regarding your own voice is, you cannot hear it accurately. As stated earlier, our ears receive our own voice sounds through an entirely different channel than the channel others hear us through.

Here is where the brain is so powerful. It often fools us into thinking we are hearing the voice we *want* to hear, and not the way it *actually* sounds. That's why the shocked words, "That can't be me!", bounce off my studio walls every time the recorder is on replay!

Now Let's Talk About the Body!

The body is the housing for all of our parts. Keeping it in perfect running condition is always the first order of business. If the body is not functioning properly, how can its contents fit into their proper place?

Every book on health will tell you what your mother has always said, "Eat your veggies, get plenty of rest, be sure to exercise, and call on Mother's Day."

At this point I won't spend time giving you a detailed health regime to follow. If you don't have one, read Oprah's book, *Make the Connection.* (This information will be covered in detail in book three of *The Wilson Voice Series* titled, *The 3-Dimensional Voice for Life,* available in your local book store soon.) It is very important however to know that proper body maintenance is vital to a healthy voice!

In the 3-Dimensional world of voice, the main function of the body is to be the physical part of this vocal equation. The body is where all that goes on in your life takes root and shows its face.

In other words, all that the mind/brain and soul put into motion will show up **somewhere** in the body.

If the programming is negative, it will show up in the voice as vocal abuse. If "All is well at the Walton's", the voice is a "happy camper."

Confronting Vocal Abuse

 There are three major physical factors that affect the voice:
- *Force: Too much force.*
- *Breath: Too little or too much breath.*
- *Pitch: Misplaced pitch.*

Any one of these three things separately can cause major abuse in the vocal parts. All of them together can mean disaster and permanent voice damage. For now, let's address them separately.

Force

When I first began my *quest for the perfect voice,* I had the honor of attending a seminar featuring Dr. Emil Froeschels, one of the great pioneers in voice research. He introduced the terms *hyper-function* and *hypo-function.* Hyper-function means too much muscular force on the voice and hypo-function means diminishing power in the muscles of the vocal organs, or weakness of the voice. One will inevitably lead to the other. Too much force weakens the voice.

This problem becomes a vicious circle that usually begins with emotional stress, and leads to tightness and gripping of the throat and larynx. This tightness results in a weak, colorless voice which lowers the pitch and allows air to escape through the cords, weakening the voice even more.

Emotions that raise the pitch:
- **Excitement**
- **Anger**
- **Hatred**
- **Fear**

Emotions that lower the pitch:
- **Sorrow**
- **Depression**

Our body physically reacts to these emotions which causes a physical reaction in our voice. Excitement will shorten our breath, and anger will tighten our throat area. Hatred will make our body close down and fear will leave us "shaking in our boots."

3 body areas affected by vocal force are:

1. Back of the Tongue: It lifts up causing a muffled, nasal sound that blocks out the bottom of the voice. The voice sounds dull with no warm lower tones to balance the nasal effect.

2. Glottis: (Space between the vocal cords) A glottal stroke is a hard attack on the glottis. It forces the vocal cords to create sound by pounding down on them and tightening the throat. The end result of this action is a strangled sound. Not much fun to listen to all day in a classroom. This is an action that can cause nodules if allowed to continue.

3. The Throat/Larynx area: Forcing this area also strangles and tightens the sound, pinches the voice, pulling the larynx up into swallow position. The pitch automatically goes up as the larynx goes up causing a thin weak sound in the voice.

All these descriptions sound exactly like my voice problem when I went to hear Dr. Froeschels speak on the advice of Roland Wyatt, an incredible voice coach and teacher I was working with at the time. My vocal problems all began with a dysfunctional, verbally abusive relationship. The cause was...

Definitely Emotional!

My Story

At the time my voice problems began, I was singing with my own band on the casino show band circuit in Las Vegas, Reno and Lake Tahoe, Nevada, doing very well career-wise, while living in a verbally abusive relationship.

As I sang my heart out every night, I was constantly bombarded by insulting remarks from an alcoholic musician. I smiled on the outside, but my voice was gripped with emotion on the inside. A few years of extreme emotional abuse caused the muscles of my larynx and vocal cords to become thick and distorted, pulling my voice completely out of its natural balance.

My vocal range began to diminish and my voice became husky and weak, forcing me to constantly push for more volume. (If too much force is put upon the voice night after night, vocal nodules can form. Lucky for me, that didn't happen.) The vocal weakness (hypo-function), however, did devastate my budding singing career and destroy my self-worth.

My situation is not uncommon among female singers. Emotional abuse, be it physical or verbal, has affected the careers of many singers from Doris Day, Billie Holiday to Tina Turner. Even today, the names of female singers on that list keeps growing.

No matter *what* your occupation may be, or what kind of abuse you are experiencing, whoever the abusers in your life may be, your boss, your spouse, your kids or a dominant co-worker, hear this well from one who has already "been there and done that"...

> (♪) *All emotional abuse be it verbal or physical, causes severe vocal stress which can cause permanent damage to your precious vocal instrument!*

I have worked for the last 20 years to undo what was brought about by misplaced emotional abuse. To this day when I find myself in an intimidating situation my "muscle memory" kicks in and my larynx starts creeping up as my voice begins pinching off my words:

I Just Hate It When That Happens!

As much as I have worked on my voice, I must constantly be on guard when it comes to my emotions. As for vocal abuse, to treat the symptoms and not eliminate the cause is absolutely useless. I could fill another book with voice horror stories, but it would accomplish nothing except to get me an appearance on The "Jerry Springer Show." Personally, I'd rather be more positive and "do" Oprah!

Breath

Emotions also affect the breath, which in turn affects the voice. (Remember: *The voice is a wind instrument.*) As your emotional temperature rises, your breath becomes shallow and rapid. The chest and shoulders tense and lift up. You can hyperventilate so much you may pass out. That's what emotions can do to your breath! Imagine how this chain reaction can tighten up your voice.

Without breath, you have no sound. In covering the subject of breath and the voice, any kind of abuse and its effects on the voice must be included.

> (♪) *Avoiding the situations that cause vocal damage can sometimes mean a career or a relationship adjustment.*

You can not fool the voice by your words. Your true feelings will be reflected in your breathing patterns even when you are sleeping.

Have you ever had one of those dreams where you are being chased and when you are caught by whatever is doing the chasing, you become terrified and try to scream, but nothing comes out? It's because you have no breath, no voice! Fear definitely constricts our breath, even in our dreams.

How breath relates to vocal abuse is through the effect improper breathing has on the voice mechanics. Faulty breathing pulls the vocal system off center and affects the way we sound.

Those who use the voice in their work must become masters of the breath or suffer the consequences with a dysfunctional sounding voice.

If you are a parent or teacher working with small children and you have faulty breathing habits that result in improper speech patterns, you could be transferring those speech patterns to your children or to your students. Remember, kids are the great imitators of the world. "What they see is what they do." In this case, "What they hear is how they talk!" Not to lay a guilt trip on you *but,* you owe it to yourself and the children in your life to fix your voice if there is a problem with your breathing that affects your speech.

Learn to Breathe Like an Actor

When you are doing any type of presentation, prepare your material, like an actor prepares for a part. Place in your scripted presentation, every breath and every pause. Use a "slash" mark between words where you want to take a breath. Always do your scripting in pencil, and give it a "run through" to see how it feels. If the breathing spots feel awkward, try another spot to breathe. This simple act of marking the breaths will slow you down and keep you from hyper-ventilating during your presentation.

Marking the Script

Try writing in your breaths and pauses like you naturally speak. Unless you are under stress, your relaxed speaking pattern has many pauses where you naturally breathe, but when placed in a panic situation, the breath is the first to go, just like in your dream.

Do not take a chance! Be a good actor and rehearse, especially where you breathe. That will help you to get the upper hand, so to speak, on voice abuse due to faulty breathing. (Go back and review the " beat, beat," exercise.) Insert a breath mark along with your beats.

Do this exercise in pencil because you may change your breath marks again and again until the breathing pattern feels right! It is very important to understand there is no right or wrong way to mark a script. It is by trial and error that you will find your "own" breathing pattern. If at first the lines make it hard to read, remember, you will be reading your breathing pattern, the rest of us will only "hear" it.

Here is your example:

Opening Story:

"Good evening fellow co-workers. (beat beat) Tonight we will talk about the effects of stress on the body. (beat) And speaking of stress, (beat beat) I met a man from shipping yesterday in the coffee room (beat) He looked real bad! (beat beat) So I asked him what was wrong. (beat) He told me he was so stressed on the job, (beat) he couldn't even sleep. (beat beat) I said, (beat) "Did you try counting sheep? (beat) He said "yeah, (beat) but that made it worse. (beat) I asked him why and he said, (beat) First he counted em (beat) then he sheared 'em, combed out the wool and spun that into cloth. (beat) He made 2 dozen suits, (beat) took the suits to New York and sold them to a wholesaler. (beat beat) He lost $5,000 on the deal and was so upset, (beat beat) he hasn't slept for a week. (beat beat) I definitely would NOT recommend counting sheep for stress/

This is a fun breath exercise that works great!

Sip the Spaghetti Exercise:

Play like you are sipping spaghetti, only instead of spaghetti, sip air. Make sure your lips are tight as you hold that imaginary spaghetti in them. Fill the lungs from the bottom up. When they are full of your spaghetti air, open your mouth and yawn-sigh the air out haaaaaaaa. Repeat the process. This is a good bathroom exercise to do before your presentation. It relaxes the breathing and if you don't have time to eat, it fills you up on spaghetti. The bonus is NO CALORIES!!!

Pitch

We have covered *force*, *breath* and now we come to *pitch*. In trying to name which one of these three is the more responsible when it comes to vocal abuse, I would have to say they are all pretty equal. However, of the three, pitch is the most *noticeable*.

We can't always detect force, and breath is an inner body thing, but pitch... boy, can we spot pitch! It has been impressed upon you over and over again in this book how important proper pitch is for avoiding voice problems.

In Dr. Morton Cooper's book, *Change Your Voice, Change Your Life*, his major focus is to teach you to find your natural pitch. In Daniel R. Boone's book, *Is Your Voice Telling On You?*, finding the natural pitch of your voice is also the first order of business. These two voice experts are in complete agreement, natural pitch is vital to vocal health.

Though both books are decidedly different and very informative, especially for someone who wants a more clinical approach to the voice, they do agree on the standard method for finding the natural pitch of your own voice.

Although there are now instruments to measure your natural pitch, the old "um-hummm" test is the easiest and it's just as reliable.

The "Ummm-hummmm test"

Have a friend ask you a question and simply answer spontaneously without thinking of the pitch of the voice. Say "umm-hummm" with your lips in a closed position.

That's it!! I told you it was simple!

Where your voice lands on the " hummmm," (not the ummmm, but the hummm) is the natural pitch of your voice. That's where you should be placing the majority of your "talking" during the working hours to avoid voice damage and strain on the vocal cords.

Here are some questions to ask yourself:

After each question say umm-hummm and take note where the pitch of your voice sits on the hummmm. You'll find the hummm is slightly higher in pitch than the ummm.

The Question?

1. **Did you enjoy this book?**
   Say umm-hmmmmm.

2. **Did you learn a lot about your voice?**
   Say umm-hmmmm.

3. **Did you find it witty and informative?**
   Say ummm-hmmmmm.

4. **Are you going to buy copies and give them to all of your friends?**
   Say ummmm-hmmmm.

The Answer!

5. **Now say *umm-hummm* and follow it by saying "hello" in the same pitch.**

6. **Now say *umm-hmmmm* followed by your name. For Example:**

Ummmm hummmm, my name is Joni Wilson and I am speaking in my natural voice pitch. How do you like me so far?

And that's the natural voice test.
Now you try it!

As simple as this is, it shows you exactly where your voice pitch should be to avoid vocal abuse.

It usually sits a bit higher than where we would like it to sit. But most people will not even notice the difference and the pressure it relieves off of your vocal cords is well worth it.

If you are a guy and your natural voice sounds like Mickey Mouse, a good speech therapist can do wonders for you. Otherwise, for the health of your voice, try to stay in your natural pitch as much as you can.

Natural Voice Pitch Awareness Exercise:

Start this exercise by placing the finger of your right hand on the abdominal diaphragm and do a few "panting breathes" to get the old pump going.

When your pumping action is going smooth, add a "haaa" to your out-going breath. (Be sure you always start by inhaling so the sound can ride out on a strong "beam" of air.)

Now inhale from the bottom of your lungs and slightly push in on the abdominal diaphragm on the exhale as you say "ummm-hummm", inhale and repeat the process.

When you feel comfortable with the "ummmm-hummm" on the exhale, add "Ummm-humm I love your car." on the exhale. Inhale again and say "Ummm-humm the weathers fine." on the exhale. Listen for the pitch change when you are in your "natural voice."

Be aware of how the pitch of the voice sounds to your ears and how it sounds to the ears "outside of you." In order to effectively add this pitch range to your every-day life, you must accept it, or your brain will negate the process.

CHAPTER 11

Conclusion

"Tell 'em what you're going to tell 'em, then tell 'em.
Tell 'em what you told 'em, then let 'em go do it"
                                        Anonymous advice.

Here we are at the conclusion of this book. I told you *what* I
was going to tell you in the introduction, then I *told* you, and now
it's time to tell you what I told you so you can take what you have
learned and *go do it!*

Out of all the information written on the pages of this book, I
hope you will come away with a greater understanding, appre-
ciation, and most of all, respect for the human voice. With all of
the above, comes the realization that in the human symphony we
call the body, the most beautiful and versatile of all the instruments is indeed the *voice.*

♪ *You have now discovered the human voice*
is a far more complex and versatile instrument
then it is widely believed to be.

Because people know so little about the voice, it swims in a
sea of speculation. This book fills in many of the blanks and puts
to rest most of those misplaced beliefs about the voice.

Voice is the communication tool you will be using for rest of your life and to be without it is one of life's great tragedies. Love and respect your voice as you love and respect your eyesight and your hearing.

Do the things you know will improve the performance of your voice, and avoid people and situations that abuse the voice.

It's vital you have a good working knowledge of what can go wrong with the voice and how to fix it.

If you wish to advance your voice studies, find a good voice coach and read the books listed in the bibliography located in the appendix of this book. If you have any major voice problems that can not be corrected through reading about the voice and the exercises given here, find a good speech pathologist. Preferably one who is certified as a clinical audiologist by the American Speech-Language-Hearing Association (ASHA.)

> ♪ *Remember: It is impossible to know your own sound . It takes another's ear to hear it correctly. So when it comes to voice, four ears are definitely better than two.*

If your life's passion has been to sing, find a good voice teacher and give yourself the gift of song. Do not fall into the "I couldn't carry a tune if it were in a paper bag" trap. If singing is in your heart, go for it! I have vocal students who are lawyers, teachers, doctors, and people from all walks of life. Singing is one of the best stress relievers there is. Now, with Karaoke music, you can have sing-along parties in your own home. You don't have to hang out in bars to be a "lounge singer". Music lifts up the spirit and feeds the soul.

There is a Bonus!

When you improve the singing voice, you add strength and resonance to the speaking voice. After all, they are the same instrument and come from the same place. Singing is simply elongated, melodic speech. The singing voice takes exaggerated air which automatically improves your breathing. Strengthening and developing the abdominal and pelvic diaphragm muscles for singing will do wonders to strenghten your speaking voice.

If you men still have problems getting to that "resonant bottom" of your lower voice, join the choir at church and live in the bass section for awhile. You can practice your pelvic diaphragm technique where it is safe and fun. Remember, where you speak in the voice range is often a learned response. A habit so to speak, and all habits can be broken with persistence, understanding and patient work.

> ♪ *Complaining about the voice is also a habit, a bad habit! To constantly complain and never do anything about it is also a boring habit. With a little work you CAN change the sound of your voice, if you truly want to!*

All of the tools to make a change are available to you in this book, and the journey is fun and rewarding. There is also an exercise tape that goes through each exercise in the book so you can "hear with the ear" the way it should be done. (There is an order form in the appendix section.)

To have a voice that is pleasant to listen to, no matter what your profession might be, is a gift you not only give to yourself, but to all who hear you. Take the time and do the work,

(the exercises). Create for yourself the best voice you can. Remember, everyday you are judged by the sound of your voice and to have the best possible sounding voice, **that voice must be moving in all three directions. Down (depth) across (width) and out (length).**

When you have mastered this technique and created a voice that can travel at will in all 3 directions, from the DEPTH of the body (1st Dimension), over the WIDTH of the emotions (2nd Dimension), and out the LENGTH of the breath (3rd Dimension), you will be the proud owner of:

The

3-DIMENSIONAL

VOICE!

Appendix

Here are some fun "rhythmic" phrases to practice:

Each list is grouped under the number of syllables in the sentence. Speak aloud each sentence in the group. Notice how each one has a rhythmic pattern according to the number of syllables in that particular sentence. Rhythmic speaking has it's own unique sound: (Some people call it "Rap.")***

Three syllables:

Yes and no.
Read the book.
What's your name?
Time to go.
Who is it?
Good evening.

Four syllables:

The train is late.
Salt and pepper
Nice to see you..
Maybe later.
Toast and butter.
How much is it?
Pleased to meet you.

Five syllables:

Turn off the iron.
The oven is on.
Flowers need water.

Six syllables:

That's a good idea.
Leave the window open.
He can phone us later.
The puppy is playful.

Seven syllables:

The top of the jar is stuck.
My dad will arrive at nine.
What shall we have for dinner?
Please give it to me again.

Eight syllables:

I love sleeping late on Sunday.
Pie and ice cream sound delicious.
I can't remember the number.

Nine syllables:

There are three bathrooms on
the first floor.
Kathy brought the vegetables
for dinner.
They all went skiing on the weekend.
Have you gone to the movies lately?
I will be glad to meet you Tuesday.

Ten syllables:

Oh no, I think I left my
keys inside.
The bakery bread smells
simply delicious.
This is the end did you have
a good time?

***Source: Professional Voice, Robert T Sataloff: Raven Press. New York

BIBLIOGRAPHY

Appleman, Ralph D. *The Science of Vocal Pedagogy*
Bloomington: Indiana University Press, 1967.

Boon, Daniel R. *Is Your Voice Telling On You.*
San Diego: Singular publishing Group, 1991
.

Brodnitz, Friedrich S. M.D. *Keep Your Voice Healthy.* Boston: Little brown and Company,1988.

Campbell, Don. *The Mozart Effect.* New York: Avon Books 1997.

Cooper, Morton, Dr. *Change Your Voice, Change Your Life.* New York: Harper and Row Publishers, 1985
.

Glass, Lillian Ph.d. *Talk To Win.*
New York: The Putnam Publishing Group,1987.

Jones, Chuck. *Make Your Voice Heard.*
New York: Backstage Books1996.

Sataloff, Robert T. *Professional Voice: The Science and Art of Clinical Care.*
Raven Press, New York 1991

Index

About the Author

Joni Wilson

Joni Wilson has managed to achieve the perfect balance of both the business and creative worlds in her colorful career. With a father in real estate and a mother with a "flair" for show business, Joni learned early in life to wear two hats. As a business woman, she achieved success in real estate, became president of a construction company, owned and reno vated a hotel in Colorado and has earned recognition as a top voice and performance coach. She is a speaker, seminar leader and author of *The Wilson Voice Series*. (See page 225 for details.)

Wearing her creative hat as a professional singer/entertainer, Joni worked the top hotels in Las Vegas, owned and operated her own dinner theater, created a jazz vocal trio, hosted a TV talk show, performed stand up comedy at the Comedy Store, and was once an opening act to Elvis.

Still wearing those two hats, Joni currently sings with a 17 piece swing band and recently record a CD of Big Band favorites. She and her partner own and operate "Productions 4 U", a company specializing in custom entertainment. As a voice and performance coach, Joni still has a waiting list of eager students.

(For additional information you can reach Joni at her Email address: joniwilsonvoice@home.com)

Words to describe Joni Wilson's *3-Dimensional Voice Method* are "best said" by her students:

"Absolutely amazing are the positive effects Joni has had on my son and daughter. Her energetic, encouragement and belief that every student is a musical "miracle-in-the-making" have motivated them to achieve levels of success and vocal competence that simply amaze me.'

Beverly Peterson
Teacher/mother

"I owe half of my voice to God and the other half to Joni. I know her method differs from conventional voice teachers, but it really works! I would never be the professional I am today without her. Not even close!"

Andrea Ceniceros
Professional Singer/actress

"I came to Joni because I needed an outlet from my stress filled job as an engineer. I wanted to improve my singing voice but what I got was a speaking voice that was no longer boring and wonder of wonders people listen to, thanks to Joni's amazing technique.

Edward Craig
Engineer

"Joni Wilson is unsurpassed as a voice teacher. In the years my son has taken lessons from Joni, I have been very impressed with her outstanding teaching methods which are reflected in my son's improved vocal skills."

Dr. Chris Schindlr
M.D./mother

"In the 5 years I have been training with Joni Wilson, her techniques have tremendously improved my singing and speaking voice. Joni's's skillful teaching methods amaze me. Working with Joni has definitely helped me to "Be my best on stage.!""

Michael Bommarito
Professional Actor/singer

The Wilson Voice Series

On the journey from birth to death, a human being will experience periodic changes in the physical and mental make up of the body and mind, There are many books that deal with aspects of the human anatomy guiding us through this process, but to date, very little has been written about the progression of the human voice at a simple everyday level of understanding.*The Wilson Voice Series* is a 5 book series dedicated to the simple understanding of the human voice and it's correct application in everyday life.

The human voice is our means of communication. It's how we audibly express our wants and needs. How we tell each other of our joys and sorrows, angers and frustrations, It is also the way we tell the world about our emotional needs and even how we entertain each other. The voice is used by the rich and poor, old and young. Regardless of ethnic background or religious belief, we can all, in spite of the consequences, "voice" our opinion.To face this world with a strong, pleasing voice is the best assurance we have that our "voice" will indeed be heard.

Book One
The 3-Dimensional Voice
A Fun And Easy Method Of Voice Improvement

Book number one is the introduction to the *3-Dimensional Voice*. It is a much needed "owners manual" for the human voice, written with wit and wisdom for everybody who has one. It is full of easy to understand and apply solutions to the voice problems that challenge us, everyday. This book is for everyone who has a voice.

Book Two
The 3-Dimensional Business Voice
The Voice Of Command
How to get people to hear what you say
and do what you tell them to do!

Book number two is for the corporate/business world of voice users. It teaches business and communication voice techniques and presentation skills used by professional "spokespeople". With basic acting skills and a bit of "humor" even the dullest presentation can "come to life." This book is for everyone who stands in front of an audience and speaks.

Book Three
The Young 3-Dimensional Voice
A Step By Step Guide To buildingVocal Strength And Confidence in the Young Voice

Book number three is a must for everyone who works with children. Most of our adult voice problems begin in our early "voice development years". This book is an in-depth look at those early years. It will guide you in preparing children to correctly use their voice's. Award winning photographer Ce Ce Canton contributes over 30 photographs of young students demonstrating *The 3-Dimensional Voice* technique for children.

Book Four
The 3-Dimensional Singers Voice
A Fast And Easy Way To Sing Like A Pro

Book number four is written for singers by a singer! In analyzing hundreds of voices, Joni Wilson became an expert in instantlyecognizing voice problems and even more of an expert at "fixing" them. Along with learning to use the amazing *3-Dimensional voice* technique you will learn the styling secrets of the "pros" and how to "sing from the heart". From Shower to stage everyone who loves to sing should read this book.

Book Five
The 3-Dimensional Voice For Life
The Spirit/Mind/Body Connection To Vocal Well Being

Book number five is a labor of love. There is more to the voice than "meets the ear." The positive and negative powers of the spoken word effect our lives everyday. In this visual and uplifting book, you will learn the positive use of the voice for healing and self improvement. This book is filled with wisdom connecting the human and the spiritual side of the voice to everyday life. You will learn the true power of the spoken word and how to create what you ask for in the "real world" using that power.

Order Information

Please send me the following:

The 3-Dimensional Voice Book... $ 15.95

The 3-Dimensional Exercise Tape... $ 8.95

Name _____

Company Name_____

Address_____

City _____State_____Zip_____

Telephone_____Fax_____

How many copies?_____

Total_____

Sales tax (CA only) _____

Shipping $2.50_____

Total_____

Fax orders: **(619) 583-4635**

Postal orders: Blue Loon Press

               P.O. Box 15660

               San Diego, Ca. 92175-5660

For additional information about *The Wilson Voice Series*
Fax: (619) 583-4635   or   Email:joniwilsonvoice@home.com